Essential
Boat
Electrics

Essential Boat Electrics

PAT MANLEY

John Wiley & Sons, Ltd

Published under the Fernhurst imprint by John Wiley & Sons Ltd, The Atrium, Southern Gate, Chichester, West Sussex PO19 8SQ, England

Telephone   (+44) 1243 779777

Email (for orders and customer service enquiries): cs-books@wiley.co.uk
Visit our Home Page on www.wiley.com

Other Wiley Editorial Offices

John Wiley & Sons Inc., 111 River Street, Hoboken, NJ 07030, USA

Jossey-Bass, 989 Market Street, San Francisco, CA 94103-1741, USA

Wiley-VCH Verlag GmbH, Boschstr. 12, D-69469 Weinheim, Germany

John Wiley & Sons Australia Ltd, 42 McDougall Street, Milton, Queensland 4064, Australia

John Wiley & Sons (Asia) Pte Ltd, 2 Clementi Loop #02-01, Jin Xing Distripark, Singapore 129809

John Wiley & Sons Canada Ltd, 22 Worcester Road, Etobicoke, Ontario, Canada M9W 1L1

Wiley also publishes its books in a variety of electronic formats. Some content that appears in print may not be available in electronic books.

Library of Congress Cataloging-in-Publication Data.

Manley, Pat.
 Essential boat electrics / Pat Manley.
     p. cm.
 Includes bibliographical references and index.
 ISBN-13: 978-1-904475-17-0 (cloth : alk. paper)
 ISBN-10: 1-904475-17-5 (cloth)
 1. Boats and boating–Electric equipment. I. Title.
 VM325.M33 2006
 623.8'503–dc22
                       2006025187

British Library Cataloguing in Publication Data

A catalogue record for this book is available from the British Library

ISBN-13: 978-1-904475-17-0
ISBN-10: 1-904475-17-5

Typeset in 9/12 Swiss 721 by Laserwords Private Limited, Chennai, India
Printed in Singapore by Markono Print Media Pte Ltd
This book is printed on acid-free paper responsibly manufactured from sustainable forestry
in which at least two trees are planted for each one used for paper production.

Contents

Contents   v

Acknowledgements   ix

Picture Credits   x

Introduction   xi

The Basics   1
    Definitions and formulae   1
    Electrical consumption   4
    Battery capacity   5
    Series and parallel   6

The Tools   9
    Multimeter   9
    Probe-type multimeter   9
    Polarity checker   10
    Side cutters   10
    Wire strippers   10
    Long-nosed pliers   10
    Hobby knife   10
    Various crimp terminals   10
    Crimping tool   11
    Heavy-duty crimp tool   11
    Mains soldering iron   11
    12 volt soldering iron   11
    Soldering iron stand   12
    Gas soldering iron   12
    Gas blowtorch   12
    Solder (multicore rosin)   12

CONTENTS

De-soldering tool 12
Screwdrivers 13
Cable ties 13
Insulation tape 13
Liquid insulation 13
Silicone grease 13
Cable threader 13
Clamp ammeter 14

Multimeters 15
Checking continuity 16
Testing a bulb 16
Checking DC voltage 17
Checking AC voltage 17
Checking current 17

Batteries 19
Types of battery 19
Measuring state of charge 23
Sulphation 24
Self-discharge 24
Ageing of batteries 24
Topping up lead acid batteries 26
Battery bank size 26
Battery charging 28
Multiple alternators 33

Electrical Supply 35
12 volt DC circuits 39
Engine-driven 12 volt DC alternator 41
AC 'mains' supply 45
AC from DC 51
Engine-driven AC supply 54
Generating sets 54
Fuel cells 56
Renewable energy 57

Switches and Relays 69
Switches 69
Relays 70

Connections 73
Connections 73
Crimped connections 75
Signal wire connectors 79
Heat-shrinking 80
Insulating awkward joints 80
Connections at the base of the mast 80

Wiring   83
   Tips   84
   Heavy-duty circuits   85
   Wire current ratings   87
   Installing new equipment   88

Circuits   91
   DC circuit monitoring   91
   Circuit protection   93
   Faults in an electric circuit 96

Electric Motors and Alternators   109
   Electric motors   109
   Alternators   111

Navigation Instruments   117
   Interconnection of instruments 117
   Multiplexers   119
   Installation of instruments 119
   PCs   120
   Communications radios   123

Anodes   125
   Cathodic protection   125
   Anodes   126
   Ground plates   129

Soldering   131
   Soldering irons   131
   Soldering technique   132
   Mechanical strength   133
   Unsoldering joints   134

Power Consumption   135

Acknowledgements

My first 'proper' book, *Simple Boat Maintenance*, which has been a terrific success, has served as a pattern for *Essential Boat Electrics*.

As with *Simple Boat Maintenance, Essential Boat Electrics* would not have been possible without the help and support of my wife Lynette. Photographing the 'how to do it' sequences needs two pairs of hands, one of which has been Lynette's.

Tim Davison has kept me on my toes when I didn't describe something in enough detail.

I hope this book gives you as much satisfaction in use as it has given me in its writing.

Pat Manley, Hythe, Southampton

Picture Credits

The following images have been reproduced from other sources with permission.

Yacht towing DuoGen on page 67. Reproduced by permission of Eclectic Energy Ltd.

Victron Energy Invertor on page 53. Reproduced by permission of Victron Energy.

ADH-100 Marine Fuel Cell on page 56. Reproduced by permission of Max Power.

Instructions to assemble the PL259 and the BNC convertor on page 123. Reproduced by permission of Index Marine.

BP Solar map showing approximate peak sun hours around the world on page 59. Reproduced by permission of BP Solar.

Yanmar diagrams from the Yanmar 3GM Handbook on page 114. Reproduced with kind permission of E.P. Barrus, Ltd.

Volvo Penta image on page 41. Reproduced with permission from Volvo Penta Europe.

Average daily sunshine January on pages 59 and 60. © Crown copyright, Published by the Met Office

Introduction

I've a friend whose boat's appetite for amps is minimal. He has a small solar panel, but where he keeps his boat, the sun sets at 10 am, even in the summer. He has a small wind charger, but the mooring is so sheltered it rarely turns. He has an engine, but it has no generator. He has a battery, but he takes it home to charge. Peter has a cabin lamp, navigation lights and basic instruments and he wants no more. These days Peter is a rarity.

Whether power or sail, today's boats need quite a lot of electricity, be it low voltage DC or mains voltage AC. To the majority of yachtsmen, electricity is a bit of a closed book, and I hope that it's those people who will find this book useful.

Essential Boat Electrics is not intended to be very theoretical, quite the reverse. Where a formula might be useful, I'll give it. Where a bit of theory is likely to help understanding, I'll give that too. In the main, it's a matter of simple words and simple pictures, as I find that when I'm talking to other yachtsmen, that's what they want.

To many sailors, electrics is a black art. *Essential Boat Electrics* is intended to help remove the fog of mysticism from the subject. To the purist, I may use terms that they disagree with. I had a comment about my

Electrics Companion that you can't 'consume' electric power! The correspondent may have been technically correct, but it's an expression understood by all, so that's what I use.

However, I have a word of warning – if you don't understand AC power, leave AC circuits strictly alone.

Each chapter covers a specific range of topics. I had a bit of a problem in setting their order, as I often had to write about a topic not yet covered, no matter in which order I arranged them. So, where necessary, I tell you where to look for that bit of information.

I cannot stress too much that you should make a wiring diagram of any modifications you make. You won't find the professional doing that, I guess he doesn't have time, but if you're going to keep track of things, please do take the time to make one. It doesn't have to be pretty, all it needs to do is to tell the story.

It's also very easy to procrastinate and say, 'Oh! I'll tidy it all up later.' It works OK and so you put off the evil day that you make it all neat and secure. As soon as you know it works, finish it off properly there and then, or it won't get done.

That's finished the preaching, so get on and use *Essential Boat Electrics* to help you do all those electrical jobs that you wished you had the knowledge to do.

The
Basics

To carry out most electrical work on your boat you really need very little theory. All you are ever likely to need is covered here, but in the main, all you need to know is how big a fuse needs to be, how much power an item uses, how thick a wire should be and how long you can run something from your battery.

The following formulae will allow you to calculate what you need to know.

DEFINITIONS AND FORMULAE

Resistance

Resistance is a measure of how difficult it is for electricity to flow through a wire or component. It's measured in ohms (Ω) using a resistance meter, normally found on a multimeter.

The higher the number, the more difficult it is for electricity to pass. Insulators have extremely high resistance and an open circuit has infinite resistance. An open circuit is like a switch switched off.

The lower the number, the easier it is for electricity to pass. A short circuit has no resistance at all and an extremely large current can flow. A short circuit is like a switch switched on.

There are several things worth noting about resistance:

- The longer the wire, the greater its resistance.

- Badly made or corroded electrical connections have high resistance.

- Resistance causes voltage loss along a wire.

- Voltage loss in a long wire run should not exceed 3%. On many boats the loss is as much as 10%, and this gives dim lights and wastes power. On components such as electric motors, this voltage loss can cause premature failure of the motor.

- Voltage loss can be reduced by shortening the wire or by using a thicker wire.

- High resistance causes heat.

Yachtsmen may occasionally need to calculate the effect of several resistances, so I'll cover this as well, just in case.

The resistance of several components connected in *series* (see p. 6) is the sum of their individual resistances. The same current flows through all of them. The system voltage acts over the complete string of components. ($R = R1 + R2 + R3$, etc.).

The resistance of components connected in *parallel* (see p. 6) is a little more complex and is found by: $R = 1 / (1/R1 + 1/R2 + 1/R3$, etc.). For only two resistances this is simplified to: $R = R1 \times R2 / (R1 + R2)$.

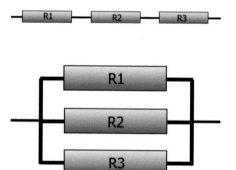

Voltage

Voltage drives the current through the wire. It's measured in volts (V) using a voltmeter.

For a particular piece of wire, a large voltage can drive a large current and a low voltage can drive a small current. For our uses, mains voltage is either 240 volts (Europe) or 110 volts (USA) and boat voltage is either 12 volts or 24 volts, depending on the boat.

Current

Current is the flow of electricity through the wire. It's a measure of the number of electrons flowing per second, but we don't stand there counting electrons. It's measured in amps (A) using an ammeter, but, just to be confusing, most formulae use *I* to indicate current. So a current (*I*) has a value (A) amps.

12 volt electronic instruments consume about 250 milliamps (mA) – that's 250 one-thousandths of an amp, i.e. ¼ amp. 12 volt fridges or radar consume about 4 amps each. A 240 volt mains electric kettle consumes about 8.7 amps, while the mains connector to the shore power will handle about 15 amps.

If you had a 12 volt shore connection handling the current (rather than the 240 volt/15 amp mains connector), the connection cable would be handling $20 \times 15 = 300$ amps and you'd need a very hefty cable. That's why we use high voltage for transmission cables.

There's a constant relationship between the voltage, current and resistance in any component and this relationship is called *Ohm's Law*. Ohm's Law tells us that the current through a wire is calculated by dividing the voltage by the resistance. Thus:

$$I = V/R$$

$$V = I \times R$$

$$R = V/I$$

Power

Power is the amount of electricity being taken at any one instant of time by a component. It's measured in watts and is calculated by multiplying the voltage by the current.

$$\text{Power} = VI \text{ watts}$$

For instance, a mains electric kettle might be 2000 watts (2 kilowatts) (240 volts $\times$ 8.3 amps) and a 12 volt fridge might be 48 watts (12 volts $\times$ 4 amps).

ELECTRICAL CONSUMPTION

What we store in our batteries, or what we pay the electricity company for, is the amount of power for however long we are using it. A light switched on for a short time costs us less than if we leave it on for a long time. Our navigation lights running all night will deplete our batteries much more than if they're on for only a couple of hours of evening sailing.

For mains electricity this quantity is normally expressed in 'units' or kilowatt hours – the power of the item multiplied by the number of hours for which we are using it. A 2 kW electric fire switched on for 2 hours would use 4 kilowatt hours (2 kW × 2 hours = 4 kW hours).

For low-voltage DC circuits, as found on boats, we express it a little differently: the number of hours it's switched on multiplied by the amps flowing. Thus, for our 12 volt radar, consuming 4 amps and running for 8 hours, it's consuming 32 amp hours (4 amps × 8 hours = 32 amp hours). Therefore, a 100 amp hour battery would have had 32 amp hours removed from it by having the radar switched on for 8 hours.

We may need to be able to estimate the electrical consumption of a component but know only its wattage and voltage.

Take a 12 volt, 25 watt navigation light bulb, for instance. 25 watts supplied by 12 volts draws just over 2 amps (25 divided by 12 = 2.08 amps). That bulb, switched on for 8 hours, consumes just under 17 amp hours of electricity (8 hours × 2.08 amps = 16.64 amp hours).

Let's see why an electric windlass, for instance, might fail prematurely if its wiring has too much resistance:

- Let's say it has a maximum power of 1000 watts and should be run at 12 volts.

- The current would be 83.33 amps (1000 watts divided by 12 volts = 83.33 amps) at maximum pulling power.

- Say the resistance of the wire is such that there is a 10% voltage drop.

- The current would now be 92.6 amps if required to pull its maximum load (1000 watts divided by 10.2 volts), because it would try to maintain power by drawing more current from the battery at the reduced voltage.

- With a 20% drop, the current would be 104.16 amps.

- This would give a 25% current overload, leading to rapid failure.

For the same reason, if you had the engine running, the voltage at the windlass would be about 13.5 volts. With the engine stopped and the battery down from overnight use, the windlass voltage could easily be reduced to 10 volts or so.

Engine running = 74 amps

Engine off = 100 amps

Which windlass is going to last longer?

BATTERY CAPACITY

The voltage of a battery gives no indication of how much electricity it can store. We might connect a 12 volt, 25 watt bulb to a battery and need to know how long the battery would power the light. We'll talk more about batteries later in the book, but from our amperage formula we can deduce that the current flowing through our bulb is 25 divided by 12, which is pretty close to 2 amps.

If the bulb stayed illuminated for 48 hours before the battery was flat, we would call that battery a 96 amp hour battery, because 2 amps flowing for 48 hours is 2 × 48 = 96 amp hours. If we ran four bulbs at the same time, the battery would last only a quarter of the time; in other words, 8 amps for 12 hours still equals 96 amp hours.

So, the capacity of a battery (to store electricity) is measured in amp hours. It's not quite as simple as that, as the amp hours capacity will vary according to the value of the current taken, but the principle holds good. As the battery ages, its capacity will fall, and when the capacity falls too much, it's time to throw the battery away.

But that's enough about batteries for now.

SERIES AND PARALLEL

Connecting in series

If we join components in line, holding hands as it were, we call this a *series* connection. For this type of connection:

SERIES

- the same current passes through all the components;

- the system voltage is applied across all of them together, so none experience the full system voltage.

Connecting in parallel

If you hold everyone else's left hand with your left hand and everyone holds everyone else's right hand, you will all be joined in *parallel*.

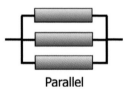

Parallel

Generally, we needn't get too excited about this, unless we are joining a couple of batteries together.

Join two 12 volt, 100 amp hour batteries in series and you get ONE 24 volt, 100 amp hour battery,

Join the same two 12 volt, 100 amp hour batteries together in parallel and you get ONE 12 volt, 200 amp hour battery.

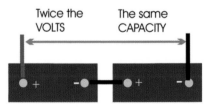

SERIES

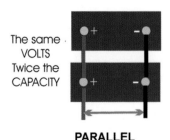

PARALLEL

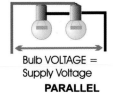

Bulb VOLTAGE =
Supply Voltage
PARALLEL

Bulbs in the same circuit need to be joined together in parallel.

Join two 12 volt bulbs in series in a 12 volt circuit and they will be pretty dim! But if you find a couple of 6 volt bulbs and need to use them in your 12 volt system, join them in series and they'll work fine.

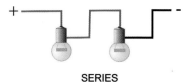

SERIES

If you need the formulae to work out more complex circuits, you'll find them in the library.

The Tools

If you are going to carry out any basic electrical repairs, installation or troubleshooting, a suitable electrical toolkit is needed. For convenience, it's probably a good idea to keep this separate from your normal tool kit.

Installing instruments may also require some additional tools, such as hole-saws to cut mounting holes in instrument panels and an electric drill and drill bits.

MULTIMETER

When troubleshooting, a multimeter is almost essential.

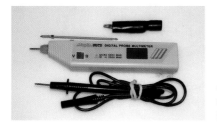

PROBE-TYPE MULTIMETER

A probe multimeter is less versatile but more compact, and has the advantage that as one probe is the meter itself, it can be used in awkward places.

POLARITY CHECKER

If you haven't got an on-board polarity checker, this is essential every time you connect to shore power. It is also essential if you are going to fit any mains sockets.

SIDE CUTTERS

The best tool for cutting wire. With care, they can also be used for stripping wire, but you have to hold the handles just so that they will cut the insulation and not the wire.

WIRE STRIPPERS

The only really satisfactory way to strip insulation from wire. Use the correct size 'notch' or you will sever some of the wire's strands, increasing its electrical resistance and weakening the wire.

LONG-NOSED PLIERS

Ordinary pliers are just too blunt-ended for electrical use. The long, tapered long-noses are indispensable for many electrical jobs.

HOBBY KNIFE

Used for many odd cutting jobs. You will need this for cutting insulation on heavier cable where it isn't cost effective to purchase a bigger wire stripper. However, do very careful not to cut through inner insulation where there's a sheath over multi-strand insulated wire.

VARIOUS CRIMP TERMINALS

The most versatile method of making electrical joints.

CRIMPING TOOL

The only proper way to make crimped joints – the cheap crimping pliers are not good enough for making proper joints. A ratchet crimping tool is the type to use. There are different makes of crimp terminals, so it's best to buy the crimper and the terminals from the same source.

HEAVY-DUTY CRIMP TOOL

If you have to crimp up some heavy-duty terminals and don't have the luxury of an expensive heavy-duty crimper, then this little beauty called the Crimpace by Tyco Electronics is much cheaper and can have the pressure applied either by a hammer or in a vice.

If you can take the wire to a vice, insert the wire into the terminal and then squeeze the crimper in the vice until the tool's end-stops touch. Make sure you hold the wire firmly in place in the terminal as you close the vice.

If you have to use a hammer, rest the crimper on a firm surface. This is probably a two-person job: one to hold the wire and terminal and the other to do the hammering. You will need good teamwork!

MAINS SOLDERING IRON

If mains power is available, a 25 watt mains iron is an asset. If you have heavier work to do, a 100 watt iron is necessary. See the chapter 'Soldering' for technique.

12 VOLT SOLDERING IRON

For use on board when no mains power is available, a 12 volt iron will do all that a mains one will do. However, it will take 2 amps at 12 volts, so you won't want to leave it on for long periods.

SOLDERING IRON STAND

You need somewhere to put the hot iron whilst you are using it. Some irons have a hook on the handle, so that you can hang them up somewhere safe. Probably a better bet is a purpose-made stand with a heavy base that can't tip over.

GAS SOLDERING IRON

For jobs where electricity isn't readily available, a gas soldering iron is a big asset. A professional one is a much better tool than its cheaper rivals, which, in my experience, suffer from rapid failure of their catalytic element. Although these 'irons' can have a naked flame if required, for soldering, the gas burns without a flame on a catalytic element, just as in a catalytic heater. This element heats the soldering tip. A rope-cutting heated tip is normally supplied as well.

GAS BLOWTORCH

For soldering heavy items, including starter cable, a gas blowtorch, as used by plumbers, will do the job. However, they produce a lot of heat, can melt the insulation and are a fire hazard. In any case, heavy-duty crimping is to be preferred.

SOLDER (MULTICORE ROSIN)

Reels of solder are obtainable in different solder diameters and are used according to the size of the items being soldered. Multicore 'rosin' flux solder is the most convenient to use for electrical wiring jobs.

DE-SOLDERING TOOL

If you have to 'unmake' a soldered joint, getting rid of the molten solder before it cools and prevents the joint from being taken apart is a problem. A 'vacuum' de-soldering tool is very useful if you expect to do much 'undoing'.

SCREWDRIVERS

Many connectors have small screws, as do junction boxes and the components themselves. A range of suitably sized screwdrivers — blade and cross-head — is essential. Include a set of small instrument screwdrivers.

CABLE TIES

Cable ties of various sizes are used to tidy up and support wiring runs.

INSULATION TAPE

Insulation tape is useful for initial tidying up and for temporary insulation. It isn't suitable as a permanent method of insulation, as in the marine environment it will become loose and sticky.

LIQUID INSULATION

Liquid insulation, which can be brushed on and built up to a suitable thickness, is very useful for use in awkward spots, especially to insulate individual connections in a small multi-wire plug and socket.

SILICONE GREASE

Use silicone grease to keep moisture at bay in screwed connectors and crimp connections which have no other means of protection.

CABLE THREADER

A nylon push threader allows cables to be run through conduits and awkward places. These are available from builders' merchants.

CLAMP AMMETER

Clips onto a cable to measure the current flowing through the wire. It's not especially accurate, but can measure high currents and you don't need to make any connections. It's especially useful for checking the output of the alternator. You just need to clip it to the alternator's output cable.

Multimeters

Troubleshooting and maintenance of the electrical system are enhanced by the use of a multimeter. These meters can be purchased for a modest price from electronics stores, and for general use, an auto-range meter is probably most appropriate, although it is more expensive than a manual one. With manual multimeters you need to estimate what the value is before you test it.

A small, probe-type multimeter frees up the hands, allowing the circuit to be tested and the meter to be read simultaneously.

The meter has an internal battery and so must be switched off when not in use. If you have an analogue meter with no 'OFF' switch, make sure you don't leave it set to resistance, otherwise there will be a continuous battery drain.

CHECKING CONTINUITY

- Set the meter to resistance (Ω) (and a low range for a manual meter).

- Hold the probes together in contact to check for a zero reading and a 'beep'. Analogue meters need to be 'zeroed' at this stage – if it can't be zeroed, the internal battery is low.

- Switch the circuit 'OFF'.

- Put the probes at each end of the wire to be tested. The resistance should be zero but will probably read several ohms because of the resistance of the wire.

- If set to 'bleep', you will get an audio warning of very low resistance for a continuity check. A 'blinking' reading indicates an open circuit (i.e. a break).

- If the length of circuit is longer than the probe wire, use a long length of wire to extend the probe (keep a long length of 10 amp wire especially for the purpose.) This allows a long single conductor to be checked.

- Measurement of the resistance of a *component* can be made only with the component isolated (otherwise the rest of the circuit may influence the reading).

TESTING A BULB

Set the meter to resistance. Hold one of the meter probes on either of the bulb's contacts and the other probe on the second contact of the bulb. If there's only one contact, the second is the metal neck of the bulb. The meter should read only a few ohms (the resistance

of the filament). If the bulb has failed, the meter will 'blink' or have a very high reading.

Fluorescent lamps can't be tested with a meter.

CHECKING DC VOLTAGE

- Switch the circuit 'ON'.

- Set to Volts DC.

- Put the probes onto the two points at which you wish to measure the voltage (red to positive and black to negative).

- A minus sign in front of the voltage indicates that the red probe has been put on the negative terminal.

CHECKING AC VOLTAGE

Do not expose live AC circuits unless you really know what you are doing. An error can be fatal.

- Switch the circuit 'ON'.

- Set to Volts AC (V~).

- Hold the RED probe to the positive wire (terminal) and the BLACK probe to the neutral wire. The meter will read the volts at that point.

CHECKING CURRENT

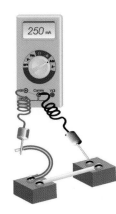

The circuit will have to be broken so that all the current flows through the meter. It will measure only DC current. A multimeter will measure only small currents, as the current has to pass through the meter and the probe wires.

- Select Amps DC.

- Put the red wire into the mA socket or 10 amp socket on the meter, according to the current expected. If in doubt, start with 10 amp.

- Switch the circuit 'ON'.

- Put one probe on the wire, the other on the terminal.

- The act of measuring the current will alter the current flow, so it's only an approximation.

Note:

- The non-electronics user has little need to measure current.

- Measuring alternator output needs a dedicated ammeter. A clip-on meter, although not very accurate, is ideal for troubleshooting.

Batteries

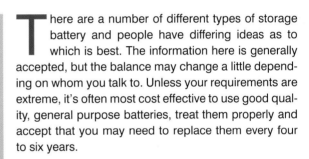

There are a number of different types of storage battery and people have differing ideas as to which is best. The information here is generally accepted, but the balance may change a little depending on whom you talk to. Unless your requirements are extreme, it's often most cost effective to use good quality, general purpose batteries, treat them properly and accept that you may need to replace them every four to six years.

A battery consists of a number of standard 2 volt (lead acid) cells joined in series in one battery case to make 'nominal' voltage.

TYPES OF BATTERY

Lead acid batteries

The standard 12 volt battery consists of six 2 volt cells. Each cell has a series of positive and negative plates suspended in a solution of sulphuric acid. The plates are kept apart by separators. Under load, electrons flow from the negative plates to the positive plates, and under charge, the flow is reversed. The amount of electricity that the battery can hold is determined by the surface area of the plates. So, a big battery will store more electricity than a small one. But that's not the whole story.

If a battery is required to give a very high current for a short time, such as when starting a diesel engine, the plates must be very thin so that the stored electricity is available at the surface of the plates very rapidly. These plates are fragile, and if a lot of electricity is taken from them, the plates will buckle. Also, they don't like vibration.

If relatively low currents are required, plates can be much thicker. They are much more robust but won't give high currents, because the electrons can't flow from deep in the plate fast enough.

The physical size of the battery is determined by how much electricity it stores (its capacity) and how quickly the electricity is required. A battery's capacity will decline slowly as it ages. Battery capacity will also vary with temperature, and at 0° C is only 50% of the nominal capacity compared with that at 30° C.

Types of lead acid (flooded) battery

Engine start battery

The engine handbook will specify the start battery's capacity in amp hours, and also its current rating (often called cold cranking amps – CCA). The current rating will be high, typically 400 amps or more, but this current is required for a very short time, and to achieve this, the plates will have to be fairly thin.

This battery is not very suitable for supplying the general domestic services of a boat, but will be discharged by only a few percent at each engine start. For this reason, the plates don't have to be very robust, as long as they can withstand the vibration.

Service battery

This will need to deliver a relatively low current, mainly between 0 and 15 amps. The plates can therefore be thicker and thus more robust. It will need to withstand much deeper discharges between charges if it's going to power the boat's services when the engine isn't running or shore power isn't available. The thicker plates will allow it to achieve this. Even so, the service

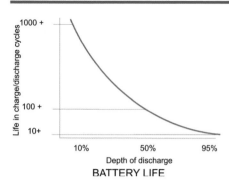

BATTERY LIFE

battery shouldn't be discharged below about 50% of its capacity, because if it is, its life will be severely reduced in terms of how many times (or cycles) you can discharge it.

General purpose batteries

Unless the demands of engine starting are severe, you can use a battery that will fulfil both engine starting and service requirements satisfactorily. It will do neither job perfectly, but the average yachtsman will probably find this type of battery perfectly OK. They are often sold as 'marine batteries' or 'heavy-duty batteries'.

Deep cycle batteries

Deep cycle batteries have much thicker plates and are heavy. The 'deep cycle' adjective doesn't mean that you can discharge the battery much more than 50%, but it does mean that you can do so a greater number of times. Unless the battery is a 'traction' battery – extremely heavy duty and designed for fork-lift trucks, golf carts and the like – it will rapidly be destroyed by fully discharging it.

Some batteries are labelled 'heavy-duty' or 'deep cycle' when in reality they do not deserve the title, and it's often difficult to get the facts. One battery company that does publish information is Optima, from Sweden, whose Optima 'Blue Top' marine battery claims to have a BCI/SAE cycle life of 350 cycles of fully charged to 100% discharged. This is an excellent figure.

Batteries should be recharged as soon as possible after being discharged in order to prolong their life.

Maintenance-free batteries

Normal batteries lose water from their electrolyte during recharging and need to be regularly topped up with distilled or ionised water. Explosive hydrogen gas is given off in this process.

If the battery has more water to start with, has its charging current restricted and is almost entirely sealed, it will not need to be topped up during its lifetime. These 'maintenance-free' batteries have no means of being topped up. They must not be charged as rapidly as a standard battery and thus will take longer to charge, but if you have a standard regulator, you won't notice the difference. A mains battery charger will need to be set for maintenance-free charging. These batteries lose very little charge during storage and should be capable of starting an engine after being stored for 18 months. A standard battery will lose up to 1½% of its charge every week it's idle.

Some so-called 'maintenance-free' batteries have caps to each cell. If it's not sealed, it isn't maintenance-free and will need to be topped up as required.

AGM batteries

The thick plates are separated by fibreglass mats which absorb the electrolyte so are virtually spill proof and very robust. They have low self-discharge rates, are classed as deep cycle and are unsuitable for engine starting. They are tolerate high charging currents.

Gel batteries

The electrolyte is in the form of a gel and the plates are thin to allow the electrolyte to diffuse into the plates. Gel batteries are sealed, so can't be topped up, and the charge voltage must be kept low so that the battery does not gas. Very strict regulation of charging current and voltage is required and gel batteries take longer to recharge than wet ones.

Nickel Cadmium (Ni–Cd) batteries

Nickel Cadmium batteries are very robust and have a very long life, but are very expensive. They can be deep-cycled thousands of times, so are very suited to use on a sailing boat. Because they lose the ability to be fully recharged unless they are fully discharged, you really need two service battery banks so that one can be fully discharged before recharging. Each bank is used alternately. Their cost is justified only if you're going to keep the boat for a long time and are going to make heavy demands on your batteries.

MEASURING STATE OF CHARGE

The state of charge (how fully the battery is charged) can be determined by means of a hydrometer, which measures the specific gravity of the sulphuric acid solution, otherwise known as the electrolyte. The battery needs time to stabilise after charge, or discharge, before the state of charge can be determined.

Generally speaking, using a hydrometer is not convenient on a boat, and the specific gravity of fully maintenance-free batteries cannot be tested. It's much easier to determine the state of charge by measuring the battery's voltage, but to do so the battery must be 'at rest'. In reality, this means that the battery needs to have been neither 'on charge' nor discharge for around 3 hours and, again, this is not very practical.

Battery 100%
state of charge

Meters that claim to be battery 'state of charge' meters just cannot work unless the battery has been at rest for 3 hours or so. In reality, they are just voltmeters with a different scale.

To get some idea of the instantaneous state of charge of your battery, you can use a voltmeter and an ammeter in conjunction. A fully charged battery at rest has a voltage of about 12.8 volts. Fully discharged, its 'at rest' voltage is about 11.8 volts. Both of these figures are reduced if a load is applied. In fact, try and start the engine with a fully charged battery and the voltage will drop to around 10 volts. Do that with a flat battery and the voltmeter will drop close to zero.

If you observe the ammeter and the voltmeter together, this table will give a fairly good indication of the battery's state of charge, even while it's being used.

BATTERY STATE OF CHARGE	BATTERY VOLTS			
	RESTED	0 AMPS	5 AMPS	10 AMPS
100%	12.8	12.5	12.4	12.2
90%	12.7	12.4	12.3	12.1
80%	12.6	12.3	12.2	12.0
70%	12.5	12.2	12.1	11.9
60%	12.4	12.1	12.0	11.8
50%	12.3	12.0	11.9	11.7
40%	12.2	11.9	11.8	11.6
30%	12.1	11.8	11.7	11.5
20%	12.0	11.7	11.6	
10%	11.9	11.6		
FLAT	11.8	11.5		

Using an amp hour meter

Another way is to use a sophisticated electronic circuit that integrates the current that has been flowing for a given time, does the sums and tells you how much has been used. With even more refinement, these meters can tell you how much charge you have put back into the battery by allowing for the efficiency of the charging

process. They are not absolutely accurate, but are very effective (though expensive).

SULPHATION

Sulphation is a natural process during discharge and recharge cycles where a layer of lead sulphate is built up on the battery's plates and this layer reduces battery performance. Sulphation can be removed only by bringing the battery back to a full state of charge, and becomes a serious problem in deep cycle batteries that rarely get fully charged. Initially soft and porous, this layer hardens with time and, once hardened, it can't be removed, rendering the battery useless. For this reason, the battery should always be left fully charged.

Some charge regulators/battery chargers have an 'equalisation' or 'conditioning' setting that can be used monthly for those batteries that are regularly deep-cycled. Because high voltages (up to 16 volts) are used, all electronics must be disconnected during equalisation and must not be used for gel batteries.

SELF-DISCHARGE

Batteries not in use will discharge themselves over a period of time. Traction batteries self-discharge at as much as 1% per day – the higher the temperature, the higher the rate. General purpose batteries are better, and sealed lead acid batteries lose only 0.1% per day.

Because of this self-discharge, sulphation will occur and monthly recharging of non-maintenance-free batteries is required when the batteries are not in use.

AGEING OF BATTERIES

Lead acid batteries will last an extremely long time if they are never discharged more than about 5%. My last engine start battery was still going strong after 12 years. Service batteries, because of their regular cycling, will slowly suffer from irreversible sulphation and their effective capacity will fall. Regularly fully charged and never discharged below 50%, you may expect five or six years, maybe more. Mistreated batteries may not last two seasons.

If one cell fails, this will pull the voltage down, not only on that battery, but also on the whole bank. If the battery bank voltage has fallen to 12.5 volts or so, after being fully charged and rested for 12 hours, you can suspect a failure of one cell. There are three ways of checking which battery has the bad cell.

- Measure the specific gravity of each cell with a hydrometer. The bad cell will have a much lower reading.

- Disconnect all the batteries. Wait about 12 hours and measure the voltage of each battery. The bad battery will still be 12.5 volts or less, the others should have recovered a little.

- Disconnect all but one battery at a time and use it to turn the engine over. You'll need to prevent the engine starting by setting the stop control to stop or by decompressing the engine. The battery that drops below 9.5 volts has the bad cell.

If the whole battery is suffering from sulphation, its real capacity will be reduced. To test this, discharge the fully charged battery by using a number of lights of known wattage for long enough to discharge it by 25% of its nominal capacity. Now measure its specific gravity or its 'at rest' voltage to determine its actual state of charge. The difference between the actual state of charge and the nominal 75% indicates the reduction in capacity.

So, for a nominal 200 amp hour battery, you want to remove 50 amp hours to reduce it to 75%. Four 10 watt bulbs on a 12 volt system would take 3.33 amps and would need to be run for 15 hours to remove the 50 amp hours. If, after 12 hours at rest, voltage is now 12.3 volts, the actual state of charge is only 50% rather than the nominal 75%. The lights have removed 50% of the capacity instead of the hoped for 25%, so the battery now has only half of its nominal capacity and it's time it was retired.

TOPPING UP LEAD ACID BATTERIES

Lead acid batteries (excluding genuine maintenance-free) need to be topped up with distilled water.

Batteries that are worked hard need attention more frequently, so start off by checking monthly and adjust the time period as necessary.

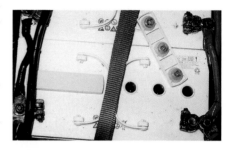

- Wipe the battery tops with a clean cloth.

- Remove the stoppers of each cell – these may be screw-in types or lift-off types.

- The liquid electrolyte should cover the plates by about half an inch (10 mm).

- Top up, if necessary, with distilled water – deionised water from a car accessory shop is the cheapest.

- Some batteries have a tube that reaches down to the correct top-up level descending from the filler neck – top up to the bottom of the tube.

- After you've finished, wipe the batteries down with a solution of bicarbonate of soda to neutralise any acid.

- Note the date that you topped up.

BATTERY BANK SIZE

Once you have calculated your likely electrical power consumption, you can start to consider the size of your domestic (service) battery bank. You need some more information before you can do this:

- How long do you wish to run without charging?

- Are you going to have a daily top-up without running your engine especially to do so?

- Do you have any other form of charging from, say, solar or wind power or a towed turbine?

- Do you have a fuel cell?

The easiest way to consider this is by illustration:

- You estimate that you have a need for 100 Ah per day.

- You will be sailing each day and anchoring at night and you have one 30 watt solar panel.

- Let us say that the engine will be running for a total of 1 hour per day, and that you have a 50 amp alternator with a 'smart' regulator. This should give you around 30 amp hours, or a little better if the battery is 'down a bit'.

- Assume that your solar panel will give 12 amp hours.

- With luck, you will have put 42 Ah back into the battery.

- This leaves a deficit of 58 Ah per day.

Now assume that you like to be out of the marina for four days, so you have a total need for 4 × 58 Ah = 232 Ah. Remember that we should not discharge our battery below 50%, so we need a service battery bank of 464 Ah. That's a lot of battery! Not only that, we now have to replace that 232 Ah.

Obviously there are a number of factors over which you have control, such as fitting a bigger alternator and adding additional sources of charging.

Another factor that can influence the size of the battery bank is that the rate of increase of charge is maximum from about 50% to 75% state of charge. If engine running is to be minimised or maximum effect from our charging source is to be achieved, then we should aim to maintain our battery's state of charge in this 50% to 75% range until we can recharge it from an external source. This means that you are effectively reducing the battery bank to only 25% of its rated capacity until you visit a marina or do a long passage under power.

On my own boat I have a 400 Ah service battery, a 110 amp alternator charging via a 'smart' regulator and two 32 watt flexible solar panels that I move around during the day to keep them out of shadow. Our use of power is modest at around 35 amp hours per day during the UK's summer, and as the solar panel can just about keep pace with the demands of our well-insulated fridge, we are just about self-sufficient. We have achieved eight days at anchor without running the engine, so I'm pretty happy with our set-up.

The biggest drain on our system is sailing at night, especially if we need to run the radar continuously, and in that situation we could have an average current draw of around 12 to 15 amps throughout the night.

BATTERY CHARGING

On a car, the alternator is used to supply the load, such as the lights and heater. The only battery charging it's designed to do is replenishment of engine starting load, which is pretty small, so if the battery gets really discharged, the car alternator is not really able to cope. This would be true on a boat that makes demands on its battery only when the engine is running. On most sailing boats the battery will need to be recharged, and this is true also on some motor boats.

Unfortunately, the charge regulator on a marine engine is just the same as on a car. The alternator output is regulated in a very rudimentary manner and its output current is forced to drop sharply after a very short time in order not to overcharge the battery. So your battery never gets fully charged, and once your battery gets moderately discharged, you can't get it back above 70% in any reasonable engine running time.

The charge entering the battery is about 90% of the area under the charging curve because of the inefficiency of converting the in-going current into battery charge. In 1½ hours' engine running you will be lucky to put 30 amp hours back into your battery with a 60 amp alternator. After 1½ hours, the in-going current will be little more than a 'trickle charge'.

If most nights will be spent connected to a shore power supply, this rudimentary charging system will be entirely adequate.

'Smart charge' regulator

The charging power of your existing alternator can be dramatically increased by fitting an external 'smart'

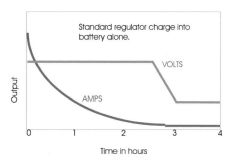

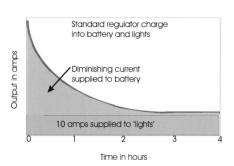

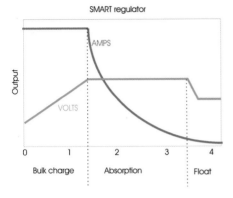

SMART regulator

Output

AMPS

VOLTS

| 0 | 1 | 2 | 3 | 4 |

Bulk charge | Absorption | Float

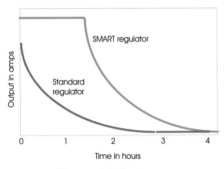

Output in amps

SMART regulator

Standard
regulator

| 0 | 1 | 2 | 3 | 4 |

Time in hours

Charge into battery

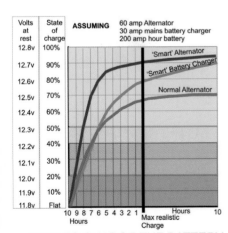

Volts at rest	State of charge	ASSUMING	60 amp Alternator 30 amp mains battery charger 200 amp hour battery
12.8v	100%		'Smart' Alternator
12.7v	90%		'Smart' Battery Charger
12.6v	80%		
12.5v	70%		Normal Alternator
12.4v	60%		
12.3v	50%		
12.2v	40%		
12.1v	30%		
12.0v	20%		
11.9v	10%		
11.8v	Flat		

10 9 8 7 6 5 4 3 2 1   Hours   10
Hours   Max realistic
Charge

TIME TO CHARGE THE BATTERY

Time to charge from 50% to 80% = 2 hours using 'Smart' alternator

regulator. Overcharging is prevented, while at the same time a high charging current is maintained for as long as it's safe, before the current tails off.

In any given time, the area under the charging curve is much greater, and the trickle charge stage is reached after a much longer time. This system will allow a battery to reach a 90% state of charge in a realistic time. In 1½ hours' engine running, our 60 amp alternator will put around 75 amp hours back into the battery, a considerable gain.

Whatever the type of regulator, the first hour of charging will give the greatest gain, because, after that, output is falling and it's not very effective to continue charging beyond 1 to 1½ hours, unless the engine would be running anyway.

However, when the battery is not fully charged, sulphation will occur, so the battery needs to be brought up to a fully charged state as frequently as possible. You need to balance maximum charging gain with sulphation and battery life to get the best possible cost effectiveness.

Charging from a mains battery charger

Cheap mains battery chargers recharge a battery in the same manner as a standard marine regulator. Unless you have plenty of time (days rather than hours) these are of little use on a boat.

Proper marine mains battery chargers work in the same manner as a 'smart regulator'. They have multiple stages of charge programme to enable the battery to be charged efficiently, i.e. to bring the battery to as high a state of charge as possible in the minimum time.

- *Bulk charge* maintains a constant current as the battery voltage increases up to the point at which 'gassing' occurs – typically 14.4 volts. Above this voltage the electrolyte begins to break down into hydrogen and oxygen gases, causing loss of electrolyte. This varies according to the type of battery and is normally set by a switch by the user.

- *Absorption charge* maintains the voltage close to the gassing point, and the charge current drops off as the state of charge rises, until the battery is fully charged.

- *Float charge* keeps the battery topped up and compensates for the battery's self-discharge. This float voltage is typically 13.5 volts.

Good battery chargers may be connected indefinitely without risk of overcharging, but do read the instructions.

At any time, the charger is able to supply any DC circuit that may be switched on, but this will prolong the time required to recharge the battery fully, especially during the bulk charge phase.

Some manufacturers refer to additional phases. In reality these are adding the inter-phase switching periods and the time supplying external loads as additional phases.

Most good chargers have the ability to run a desulphation programme, known as *equalisation*. This can harm the battery if used incorrectly, so make full reference to the charger's instructions, especially with regard to battery type, frequency of use and time the high voltage is applied.

If the requirement is to 'top up' your battery overnight, then its output in amps is as important as its programmed charge ability. For this you need to know how much you are likely to have discharged your battery or the capacity of the battery bank. Generally these two will be closely linked, so it's normal to match the charger output to the capacity of the battery bank.

A good starting point is that the charger's output should be about 10% of the battery capacity (ignore the engine start battery). If high battery loads will be applied at the same time as charging, you may need to add this extra load to the output of the charger.

If you have a 400 amp hour battery bank, then a 40 amp charger would be appropriate. If there were a continuous requirement for a further 10 amps for a fridge and a cabin heater, for example, this 10 amps should be added to give a 50 amp charger.

Charging multiple batteries

Unless the electrical system is very basic, as above, there will be at least two batteries: an engine start battery and a service (house) battery. The service battery may comprise more than one battery, but these are permanently connected as one unit. Unless they are being charged, these battery 'banks' are always separated.

There are several ways of connecting and isolating battery banks, and each method has advantages and disadvantages.

- simple manual battery switching;
- using a blocking diode;
- using an 'ignition switch' controlled electrical relay;
- using a voltage-sensitive relay.

Manual battery switching

This is the simplest and best method of connecting battery banks for charging. You have complete control, and the only downside is forgetfulness.

When you wish to charge your batteries, you decide which needs what and for how long. At the appropriate times, you make or break the various switches to control the charging procedure. This is the most efficient way of doing the job, and with proper control you can maximise battery life.

BUT, if you forget to isolate the battery banks after you stop the engine, you may not have enough charge left in the engine battery to start the engine.

Blocking diodes

Blocking diodes are solid-state, electronic 'non-return valves'. All the battery banks are connected to the

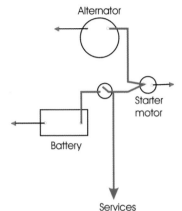

STANDARD SINGLE
BATTERY CHARGING

MANUAL SWITCHING
multiple batteries

charging system all the time, but electricity can flow in one direction only – from the charger to the battery. Electricity can't flow from battery to battery, so once the charger or alternator stops charging, the batteries are effectively isolated. Even when under charge, the batteries are isolated from one another, so it's possible to charge both maintenance-free and standard wet lead acid batteries at the same time. Being solid state means this system is very reliable and it's also completely 'fit and forget'.

Diodes have one inherent major disadvantage – there's a voltage drop across the diode's input and output terminals, so the battery gets about 0.7 volts less than the alternator's output. This prevents the battery from ever becoming fully charged. However, this problem can be overcome provided that the alternator is 'battery-sensed', i.e. that the alternator measures its output voltage at the external terminal rather than internally within the alternator. In this case, the 'sense' lead is attached to the output side of the diode, rather than the alternator's output terminal. The alternator will now produce more volts to compensate for the drop across the diode and the battery can become fully charged.

Ignition switch controlled charging

When the ignition switch is turned on, a relay is energised and the battery banks are connected for charging. With the ignition off, the battery banks are isolated.

While this sounds very simple, the disadvantage is that should you forget to turn off the ignition (some Volvos, for example, do not sound an alarm when the engine stops but the 'ignition' is still on), the batteries will continue to be connected, with the danger that the engine start battery may become discharged. Should the contacts stick, the battery banks will not isolate and, similarly, if the alternator fails, isolation will not occur until the ignition is switched off.

The relay's electromagnetic coils will take some power to hold the contacts closed.

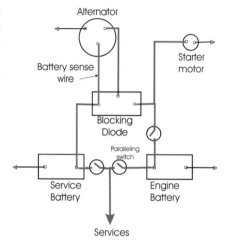

BLOCKING DIODE
SPLIT CHARGE

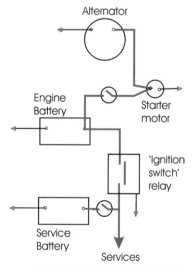

'IGNITION SWITCH' CONTROLLED
SPLIT CHARGE

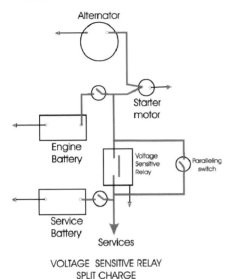

VOLTAGE SENSITIVE RELAY
SPLIT CHARGE

Voltage-sensed relay

An electronic device operates the relay to connect the batteries together for simultaneous charging when it senses a rise in voltage, indicating the application of a charging source. When the charging voltage is removed, the device isolates the batteries. Connect and isolate voltages are sometimes user-selectable and they may protect against too high a charging voltage. Such a device is Heart Interfaces' *PathMaker*. Simpler devices are supplied by BEP and Blue Seas.

Although there is no voltage drop across the device and it can be used with any type of alternator, it does consume a small amount of power (0.3 watts–25 milliamps) when the batteries are isolated and there's no charging current.

Dual sensing VSRs allow any charging source on either battery to charge the other battery by combining the two. Useful if you have a mains battery charger or wind or solar charging.

Method used	Advantages	Disadvantages
Simple manual battery switching	Very simple. Cheap	You may forget to do the switching. Engine battery may then become discharged.
A blocking diode	Fit and forget Can charge different types of wet lead acid battery at the same time. Medium cost.	Can't use with 'machine-sensed' alternators.
An 'ignition switch' controlled relay	Fit and forget. Cheap	Must remember to switch 'ignition' off.
A voltage-sensitive relay	Fit and forget. Can also sense other charging sources such as a battery charger.	Uses a small amount of power when 'off charge'.

MULTIPLE ALTERNATORS

The easy way of harnessing the output of multiple alternators, either two alternators on one engine or separate twin-engine installations, is to have each alternator supplying separate battery banks.

A standard twin-engine installation has separate battery banks for each engine, with a temporary switch to join the banks together for engine starting should one battery be flat. This may be satisfactory when little demand is made on the batteries. It's a waste of alternator output if one alternator is charging its engine start battery while the other is charging the bigger service battery.

Because each alternator will have a slightly different output, it's not a good idea to join the two sets of batteries directly together, except for emergency engine starting. In this case, it's best to use a multiple-input split charge diode. This way, both alternators are charging all the batteries, but each battery bank is isolated from the others and each alternator is isolated from the other.

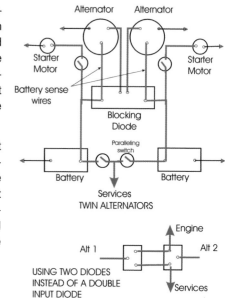

Alternator   Alternator

Starter Motor   Starter Motor

Battery sense wires

Blocking Diode

Paralleling switch

Battery   Battery

Services

TWIN ALTERNATORS

Engine

Alt 1   Alt 2

USING TWO DIODES
INSTEAD OF A DOUBLE
INPUT DIODE

Services

Electrical Supply

P ower generation is always going to present a headache on a boat, unless it's permanently connected to a mains supply alongside.

The various elements of the electrical supply are inter-linked in such a complex way that they need to be considered as one. How you interlink them will depend on how you use your boat and the demands put on the electrical system. The various elements are:

- engine-driven DC supply;
- wind-driven DC supply;
- solar panel DC supply;
- towed water generator DC supply;
- engine-driven AC supply;
- auxiliary on-board 'generator set';
- AC 'mains' supply.

These supplies are all intermittent, so an essential in the supply chain is an electrical storage battery.

A sailing boat differs from a motor cruiser only when underway, in that the motor cruiser will be generating electricity and the sailing boat often will not. Once they are moored or at anchor, they are equal.

Generally, new boats have only the most basic electrical supply system. The owner will have to upgrade the system if he is going to spend much time away from shore support. Even the boat's shore AC supply system is often an 'extra'. The only logical way to determine how, if at all, you need to upgrade your system is to calculate your electrical requirements. This requires two pieces of information for each item: how much power it consumes and how long it's switched on.

Then you need to see how the requirements compare with what electricity is available, if any, at the time you need it. This allows you to see if the requirement can be matched by a generation source, such as running your engine, or if electricity will need to be 'stored'.

You don't necessarily need to supply all your demands from the generating source. What you do need to do is to determine how long you wish to be able to run from your batteries before you need to recharge them from a 'primary' source, such as running the engine or shore power. Your 'secondary' charging sources just need to prevent your battery falling below a 50% state of charge in that time interval.

Power requirements underway – 8-hour trip

Item	watts	amps	hours	Ah/day	Duty cycle
Underway, Day, DC					
Instruments	3.6	0.3	8	2.4	
Radar	25–50	2.5–4.0	3	7.5–12	
Chart-plotter mono	3.6	0.3	8	2.4	
Chart-plotter colour	12–24	1–2	8	8–16	
Fridge	50	4	3	12	33%
VHF/DSC radio	3.6	0.3	8	2.4	
CD player/radio	12	1	2	2.0	
Autopilot	24–72	2–6	8	6–18	33%
Typically 40 Ah for 8-hour trip					
Underway, Day, AC					
Laptop computer	50	4	8	32	
Microwave	500	42	0.1	4.2	
Typically 36 Ah for 8-hour trip					

continued

Item	watts	amps	hours	Ah/day	Duty cycle
Underway, Night, DC					
Cabin light (1 × 10 watt)	10	0.3	8	2.4	
Nav. lights (1 × 25 watt)	25	2	8	16	
Instruments	10	1	8	8	
Radar	25–50	2.5–4.0	3	7.5–12	33%
Chart-plotter mono	4	0.3	8	2.4	
Chart-plotter colour	12–24	1–2	8	8–16	
Fridge	50	4	3	12	33%
VHF/DSC radio	3.6	0.3	8	2.4	
CD player/radio	12	1	2	2.0	
Autopilot	24–72	2–6	8	6–18	
Typically 60 Ah for 8-hour trip					
Underway, Night, AC					
Laptop computer	50	4	8	32	
Microwave	500	42	0.1	4.2	
Typically 36 Ah for 8-hour trip					

A modern cruiser could easily consume 115 Ah for a 12-hour passage under sail. Frugal use of electrical power could reduce this to 35 Ah by using only essentials, such as navigation lights and instruments.

Power requirements moored for 16 hours – self-sufficient

Item	watts	amps	hours	Ah/day	Duty cycle
Moored, Day, DC					
Fridge	50	4	16	21	33%
CD player/radio	12	1	3	3	
				24	
Moored, Day, AC					
Laptop	50	4	0.5	2	
Microwave	500	42	0.2	8	
				10	

continued overleaf

Moored, Night, DC					
Cabin lights (4 × 10)	40	3.6	3	11	
Anchor light (1 × 10)	10	1	8	8	
CD player/radio	12	2	1	2	
Fridge	50	4	3	12	33%
TV	50	4	2	8	
				41	
Moored, Night, AC					
Microwave	500	42	0.1	4	
				4	

On a modern cruiser, 24 hours moored could typically consume 80 Ah. Frugal use of power could reduce this to 35 Ah per day. Additionally, if a diesel-powered heater is used, expect to consume 4 Ah per hour run.

Power requirements alongside with shore power

Item	watts	amps	hours	Ah/day	Duty cycle
DC 12 volts					
Cabin lights	60	5	4	20	
CD/radio	12	1	4	4	
TV	50	4	2	8	
Fridge	50	4	8	32	33%
				64	
AC 240 volts					
Microwave	600	2.5			
Electric kettle	2000	8.3			
Toaster	2000	8.3			
Battery charger	500	2.1			
Electric heater	2000	8.3			
Immersion heater	1500	6.3			
Total	8600	35.8			

Normal pontoon power is 15a. It is obvious that only selective use can be made of 240 volt items.

12 VOLT DC CIRCUITS

Except in the most basic boat systems, there will be at least two batteries. It is sometimes recommended that, for a twin-battery system having two batteries of the same capacity, alternate use is made of each battery for engine starting OR supplying the boat's services. This is to ensure equal life for both batteries. I don't go along with this method, as a battery used only for engine starting will last a very long time and engine starting is thus assured, which, to my mind, is very important. The other battery, which has constant discharge/charge cycling will not last as long, but its failure will not be as important and can be anticipated. As soon as the domestic battery gets much bigger than the engine battery, this debate doesn't arise.

Thus, one battery will be reserved for engine starting only, to ensure that there will always be sufficient electrical charge to start the engine. The other will be used to run the boat's services, such as lighting, instruments, radio, etc. This means that the engine circuit and the service (domestic) circuits are isolated. Some form of temporary connection will be required when charging the batteries (see Charging multiple batteries on p. 28, and the figures on p. 38) and for emergency starting should the engine start battery become discharged.

Battery switches

Switches are required so that circuits can be isolated from their batteries as a safety measure. A switch will also be necessary to combine the circuits for charging and emergency starting. These switches may be required to carry in excess of 300 amps in the case of engine starting, so high-quality, heavy-duty switches are required. Not all cheap switches meet the high-quality requirement, and wear may cause the circuit to break unintentionally. This can cause expensive damage to the alternator if the engine is running.

A common type of switch is the 'OFF-1-BOTH-2' battery switch, but this has a serious disadvantage on boats fitted with voltage-sensitive electronics such as a GPS.

During engine start, the voltage on the engine battery may well fall to a value below that at which the GPS automatically switches off. The problem is that, however the switch is set, when wired conventionally, the engine starter motor AND sensitive instruments are all supplied by the same battery while the engine is started.

Many production boats suffer from this problem, and a modification should be made. This comprises supplying the services direct from the battery via an isolation switch, rather than from the existing switch, which is then used only for determining which battery is used to start the engine.

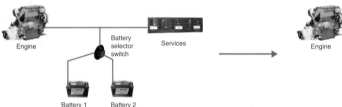

In fact, rather than fitting an 'OFF-1-BOTH-2' switch, three separate heavy-duty 'ON–OFF' switches are a better option.

An 'ignition switch' controlled 'battery combiner' has the same effect, in that sensitive instruments may switch off while the engine is started.

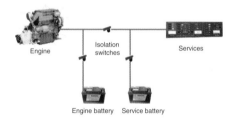

Service 12 volt DC circuit

The complexity of the service circuit will vary according to the size of the boat and the on-board systems. However, a simple block diagram can illustrate the basic principles.

The EU 'Recreational Craft Directive' (RCD) requires boat builders to supply a wiring diagram with a new boat. Some builders' wiring diagrams are derisory. Wires will commonly be red or black, and unless they are labelled, tracing wiring to various components can be difficult.

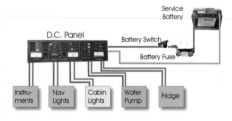

12 volt Service Circuit

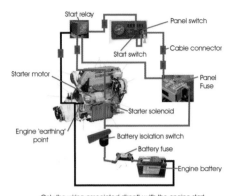

Start relay
Panel switch
Start switch
Cable connector
Starter motor
Panel Fuse
Starter solenoid
Engine 'earthing' point
Battery isolation switch
Battery fuse
Engine battery

Only the wiring associated directly with the engine start circuit is shown

Reproduced by permission of Volvo Penta Europe.

Engine 12 volt DC circuit

The engine manufacturer will have supplied a wiring diagram in the engine's handbook. Multicoloured wires are bundled in 'looms', but following the colour coding enables all wires to be identified.

Some installers are against fitting a battery fuse in the engine start circuit, because if it blows with the engine running, the alternator diodes may 'blow'. While this may be true, a fire due to a short circuit will be much more catastrophic than blown diodes. I prefer to fit a fuse.

ENGINE-DRIVEN 12 VOLT DC ALTERNATOR

Depending on the size of the engine, the alternator will usually have a maximum output of between 35 and 60 amps as standard, although it's possible to fit one of higher output. Higher outputs often require a multi-belt drive to prevent belt slip.

Modern alternators (as opposed to DC dynamos) generate alternating current (AC) and convert this into direct current (DC) to charge the battery. The voltage is regulated at a nominal 12 volts (or 24 volts) to charge the battery and supply the electrical loads.

The battery must *never* be disconnected from the alternator when the engine is running or the alternator's 'diodes' will be destroyed. In other words, DO NOT switch off the engine battery switch when the engine is running. Not all battery switches are of the same quality and unless yours is marked with a well-known maker's logo, one circuit may be broken before the next has been selected. If in doubt, don't even change the battery selection with the engine running. Some 'single' battery switches may lose contact, as they wear even when switched on.

Alternator output

You would be wrong to think that a 60 amp alternator will deliver 60 amps as a matter of course. Three things materially affect output: alternator speed, alternator temperature and the load to which it's connected.

Alternator output will depend on how fast it is turning (rpm). Any particular alternator has a maximum speed, and so its driving pulley size is calculated so that this maximum rpm is not exceeded at the engine's maximum speed. For instance, if the alternator maximum rpm was 9000 and the engine maximum speed 3000 rpm, the gear ratio would normally be chosen as 3:1.

So, if we run our engine at 1500 rpm, the alternator speed will be 1500 × 3 = 4500 rpm. Its output will be less than 50 amps. If the engine compartment is very hot, then the output may be only 40 amps. If the engine is running at idle rpm, the alternator output is little more than a 'trickle' charge.

In order to control its output, the alternator needs to know the battery voltage. On many alternators it does this by sensing the output voltage inside the alternator. This is fine if the wiring runs are short, the terminals have good contacts and there's no split-charging diode. This is known as *machine sensing*. Far better is *battery sensing*, where the output voltage is sensed at the battery terminal, because there may be a considerable voltage drop between the alternator and the battery. If this is the case, the battery can never be fully charged.

The alternator must always supply any user of electricity via a battery. The alternator is never connected directly to the 'load'. Provided that the alternator has sufficient output, it will always supply enough amps to satisfy the load. In other words, if the lights need 10 amps, the alternator will supply them with 10 amps.

If the alternator was supplying 10 amps to the lights AND charging the battery, its output would be 10 amps constant for the lights PLUS a diminishing charge going into the battery.

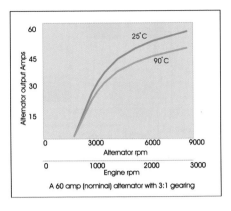

A 60 amp (nominal) alternator with 3:1 gearing

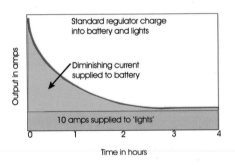

How big should the alternator be?

There are two considerations here: What is the maximum load at any one time? How big is the battery bank?

- Normal electrical loads are always satisfied from the alternator's output.

- This normal requirement may reduce the charge going into the battery.

- The alternator will never satisfy high-current loads, such as anchor windlasses and bow thrusters.

- These high loads are supplied by the battery, with the engine running at the same time to reduce battery drain and a fall in battery voltage under this load.

- There's a relationship between the alternator output and the maximum size of battery bank it can realistically charge.

Charging batteries is a complicated science, but as far as we are concerned, it's easy to use a rule of thumb which says that maximum charging current (amps) needs to be about one-third of the battery capacity (amp hours) for efficient rapid battery charging. In other words, the battery capacity should be no more than three times the alternator output.

A standard 60 amp alternator is, therefore, suitable for charging a 180 amp hour service battery bank. It's usual to discount the engine start battery, because generally it's pretty full anyway.

If you are going to have heavy use of your battery over a weekend, but then take all week to charge the battery on mains power, the size of your alternator compared to the size of the battery is not so important.

You should never allow your battery to become more than 50% discharged, as discussed in the chapter 'Batteries'.

Generally, unlike a car, the size of the alternator is dictated by the size of the battery bank. If you increase the size of your battery bank, you may need to fit a bigger alternator or a second alternator.

A bigger alternator

The standard belt drive may need to be upgraded if you fit an alternator of higher output. Its capability will depend on the contact angle of the belt, its section and its tension. A wide 'poly belt' or multiple belts may be required. I have found that the capability of a single belt can be increased by using a high-temperature belt in combination with machined pulleys, rather than the standard pressed steel type. An overworked belt will shed a lot of black dust and will fail after only a few tens of hours.

A second alternator

By fitting suitable brackets to the engine, it may be possible to fit a second alternator being driven by a second belt and pulley system.

Consult the engine manufacturer to ascertain the maximum side thrust loadings allowed on the crankshaft.

Think about how you will connect them electrically, see the section on battery charging in the chapter 'Batteries'.

Starting load

A bigger than normal load on the engine when starting from cold with well-discharged batteries may have undesirable effects, such as difficult starting or black smoke after starting. It's almost certain that you will choose to fit a 'smart' regulator if you upgrade your charging system (see battery charging in the chapter 'Batteries') and some of these have a time delay before the alternator starts to charge to overcome these problems. This is a desirable feature.

These problems can occur even with a standard system and I've recently discovered that a modification to the Yanmar 1GM10 fitted with a saildrive leg was made in 1992 but not included in the handbook. To prevent problems with cold starting, the alternator does not produce a charge until the leg's oil temperature reaches 25° C. The alternator warning light was changed to illuminate when the alternator was producing current, rather than the normal warning function. This resulted in owners having undercharged batteries if the engine was run for only a short period of time, so you need to allow for the non-charging period when charging your battery.

Voltage regulation

A standard 12 volt alternator has a varying output voltage according to the state of charge of the battery. It will

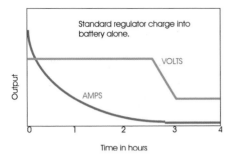

Standard regulator charge into battery alone.

VOLTS

AMPS

Output

Time in hours

charge at a constant voltage of around 14.2 volts with a diminishing charging current. When the charging current drops to a couple of amps, the voltage will reduce to about 13.2 volts. These voltages are doubled for a 24 volt system. As we have seen, this primitive system of regulation will never fully charge our batteries.

AC 'MAINS' SUPPLY

Being able to connect to a dockside mains-power system allows the use of mains-powered equipment, such as an electric kettle, and also provides a chance to charge the boat's batteries.

It is highly unsatisfactory to rely on an extension lead and 13 amp socket to supply the boat with AC power.

Any work undertaken on AC circuits by unskilled people is potentially lethal.

Normal mains AC supply is 'three wire' – live, neutral and earth – with the earth voltage at zero volts relative to earth. This is achieved by *grounding* the earth wire with a metal spike driven into the ground, hence its name.

The boat's DC ground is achieved by connecting the DC circuit's negative wire to the hull's external anode, so that the 'negative' is the same 'zero' volts as the sea (or lake or river).

The shore supply

In the UK, the shore supply socket is normally rated at 15 amps, although some marinas have a 30 amp supply available at some berths. There are usually several 15 amp sockets at each supply point, and if you exceed the rated load for your socket, you may well 'trip out' the others at that point. Often, only the marina staff can reset these circuit breakers.

It is not uncommon to find some sockets incorrectly wired so that neutral and live contacts are reversed, so fit a polarity indicator to your boat's AC control panel.

If one is not fitted to the boat's AC panel, plug a domestic 13 amp socket tester into a 13 amp socket instead.

If you find a socket incorrectly wired, inform a member of the marina staff. To temporarily overcome the problem, your 'kit' should include a polarity reverser. Some upmarket boat control panels have a built-in facility to do this. Generally though, you will need to make up your own.

In the USA, where 115 volts is the norm, some marinas have a 240 volt supply available by using two phases of the 115 volt system. This will, by the nature of the wiring, indicate that you have reverse polarity. This is due to the way the 240 volts is obtained and the way the tester works, so you don't need to use your reverser lead.

If the reverse polarity of the shore supply is not corrected, all switches are operating in the neutral wire and the positive wires are unswitched. A fault in the wiring or appliance will not operate a single pole circuit breaker and a dangerous condition can result, especially in a damp marine environment.

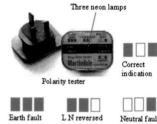

Three neon lamps

Polarity tester

Correct indication

Earth fault   L N reversed   Neutral fault

DIY polarity reverser

Make up a short shore power lead and reverse the neutral connections on plug OR socket. Mark this reversing lead clearly so that you know what it does. The cable should be of the same current-carrying capacity as your shore-power cable. If you find that the polarity of a shore-power outlet is reversed, plug your reversing lead into the shore power outlet, and then your normal shore power lead into the reverser's socket. Now check that your final polarity is correct.

The shore-power cable

If you normally plug into a 15 amp socket, your cable must be capable of carrying 15 amps. The cable size will depend on its length as well, to prevent too much voltage loss. Unless the cable is very short, it should be of 2.5 mm² section. Use outdoor (flexible) round cable with a proper plug and socket to fit the shore-supply socket and the boat's connector. If you keep the cable on a reel, uncoil all the cable before you switch on the power, or dangerous overheating of the coiled cable is possible. For this reason, several shorter cables, rather than one very long one, are probably more conven-ient.

Always connect your cable to the boat first and the shore socket last. When disconnecting, disconnect the shore cable first, so that if the end should fall into the water, the free end will not be live.

If your shore-power cable plug or socket contacts look corroded, they could be much worse on the inside!

The boat's AC circuits

AC earthing (grounding)

The shore supply is grounded ashore, and there are different schools of thought as to whether it should be connected to the ship's DC ground. On many boats there's no interconnection between the AC and DC grounds. Recommended practice at the moment is to make a connection, but corrosion of underwater fittings is then a distinct possibility.

No interconnection between shore AC ground and ship's DC ground

If the AC and DC grounds are not interconnected, the only ground connection is via the shore-supply cable. *Any failure of that ground connection due to poor joints or corroded connections could cause the casing of an appliance to become live if a fault occurs, and bring danger of electrocution to anyone touching it.*

Connecting the AC ground to the ship's DC ground

- Should an AC short to earth occur on the boat, com-plete safety is assured to its occupants as there will always be a path to ground.

- Because it's unlikely that the shore-side ground and the ship's ground will be at exactly the same voltage, stray current corrosion is likely to occur to the boat's underwater metal components.

• Should an electrical fault occur in the AC circuit sending current to the ship's ground, nearby swimmers are at risk of an electric shock.

Stray current corrosion due to the difference in voltage between AC and DC grounds can be prevented by fitting a galvanic isolator between the two. This isolates the two circuits if a small voltage difference is present (up to about 1.5 volts) but allows free conduction for larger voltages, such as when a short to ground occurs. Even then, there are disagreements as to where it should be fitted.

Isolator between AC ground and DC ground

This would seem to be the ideal position, because, except in the case of a short to ground, there is no effective connection between the grounds, and stray current corrosion will not occur due to any voltage difference between the grounds.

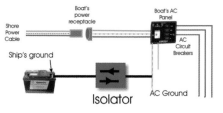

Isolator separating ship's ground and AC ground

However, if there is any interconnection between the grounds in any one piece of equipment, such as a generator set or a cheaper, non-isolated battery charger, the isolator is bypassed and may just as well not be fitted.

Provided that all AC equipment is isolated from the ship's ground, I believe that this is probably the best solution.

Isolator fitted in the ground line as it enters the ship

This effectively means that there is no ground connection to shore unless there is an accidental short to ground, so in normal circumstances, the ship's ground (anode) is the only one present. This means that any mains AC fault will be led to the ship's anode. It is safe for those on the boat, but not to swimmers nearby, if a short to ground occurs, as they could feel the full force of the mains 240 volts.

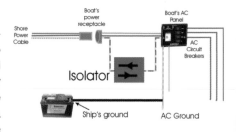

Isolator breaking shore supply ground line

As far as stray current corrosion is concerned, differences in voltage of the two grounds are avoided (because there's only one). However, it is argued that because of the resistance of the isolator, stray currents produced by on-board AC devices may actually increase corrosion to hull-mounted hardware.

If there is any chance of AC equipment having a connection to the ship's ground, this is the way to connect the isolator, but there may be increased corrosion of hull-mounted hardware.

The boat's AC wiring

Residual current devices (RCDs)

The boat's AC distribution panel should incorporate an RCD (or residual current circuit breaker – RCCB) In a circuit that is operating normally, the current flowing through the live and neutral wires is the same. If a short to ground occurs, current flows to earth, causing an imbalance in the live and neutral wires that is detected by the RCD, causing it to trip. RCDs are very sensitive, and in the marine environment, small earth leakages are common. These do not affect the operation of the appliance, but several small leakages together can cause the RCD to trip. This nuisance is often very difficult to cure and can cause the shore-side breaker to trip as well, much to the annoyance of other users.

To eliminate this problem, make sure all the terminals are clean and install them in a dry compartment. Don't install the AC shore connection or its breakers in a cockpit or transom locker because they are likely to be much damper than the inside of the cabin.

AC circuit breakers

Each on-board AC circuit should be protected by a circuit breaker. If a short circuit occurs, the high current flowing through the circuit breaker will cause it to trip. The size of the breaker, in amps, should be matched to the current-carrying capacity of the cable and the power consumption of the appliance. Normally on a boat, the shore supply will be 15 amps, which must not be exceeded by the appliances that are actually switched on at the same time. A correctly wired on-board AC circuit will use cable that will handle 13 amps (normally it will be 2.5 mm^2) so it would be usual for the

AC circuit breakers to be rated at between 10 and 16 amps. The maximum single appliance load, so that 13 amps is not exceeded at 240 volts, is 3120 watts.

Wiring electrical sockets (outlets)

Ring mains

Normal house wiring practice is to use a *ring main*. Current can be fed either way round the circuit, allowing current of double the rating of the wire, but this needs twice the length of wire. As normal domestic 2.5 mm² cable can carry 20 amps, because the current can arrive along both arms of the ring at the same time, wiring as a ring main means it can carry a maximum of 40 amps.

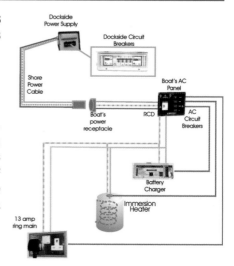

Boat's AC power circuit

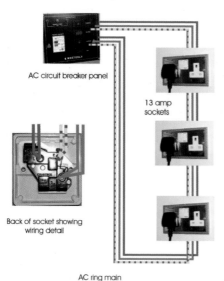

AC circuit breaker panel

Back of socket showing wiring detail

13 amp sockets

AC ring main

On a boat connected to a 16 amp shore supply, the maximum current available is less than the carrying capacity of a single 2.5 mm² cable, so running a ring main may be a waste of cable.

Spur wiring

Single 2.5 mm² cable is run from the circuit breaker to each socket. This may save cable, but if you have a lot of sockets, there will be a lot of connections to the circuit breaker. This may not be practical unless you use a junction box.

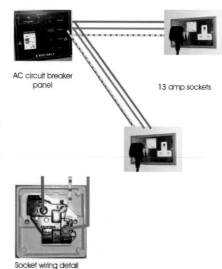

AC circuit breaker panel

13 amp sockets

Socket wiring detail

Spur wiring

Don't use domestic 'flat', single-core cable on a boat. It is too rigid and too brittle. Use 'round', multi-strand cable.

Most boats use domestic quality cable, circuit breakers and sockets in the AC circuits and these aren't designed for a marine atmosphere. You need to look out for corrosion and replace the components as necessary.

Isolating transformers

Some authorities recommend the use of isolating transformers. These are inserted between the shore supply and the boat's AC circuits, and the current is transferred from one to the other magnetically. There is no direct connection between the two.

The arguments for and against the use of isolating transformers are complex, but it is generally accepted that the use of an RCD gives excellent protection against the chance of electrocution, and fitting an isolating transformer is not common in Europe.

Test the RCD regularly by operating its test button. The circuit breaker should trip immediately the button is pressed.

AC FROM DC

When you're not tied up alongside with AC mains available, or if you haven't got an on-board generator, you can get mains AC current from your DC supply. Unless your AC demands are very modest, the drain from your batteries can be huge.

Conversion is done by using an electronic device called an *inverter*. AC voltage varies cyclically 50 or 60 times a second, and the steady voltage of a DC supply is changed into a varying voltage that resembles the AC's sine wave.

The current drawn from your DC battery is found by multiplying the AC current by the AC voltage divided by the DC voltage and dividing by the inverter's efficiency as a decimal.

MAINS ON/OFF

Circuit breaker

Test button

A 90% efficient inverter powering a 240 volt appliance requiring 10 amps will draw:

$$(240 \times 10) / (0.9 \times 12) = 222 \text{ amps}$$

Even when supplying no power, an inverter will have a small current draw from the battery, so needs to be independently switched.

Square wave inverters

These cheap inverters change DC into a very crude square waveform that is often incompatible with the AC appliance.

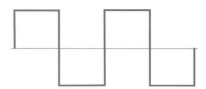

Sine wave inverters

These produce a waveform almost indistinguishable from true AC and are costly to produce, but will run any AC device.

Quasi-sine wave inverters

These form a 'half-way house' (often called modified sine wave). Some produce near sine wave AC, while others are much closer to a crude square wave, especially under load. Price is usually an indication of sine wave quality, but not always so. Sensitive electronic equipment, such as TVs and stereos, can be upset by poor sine wave quality. Ensure that the inverter you buy is compatible with its intended use.

Small, portable inverters, up to about 350 watts

These are usually plugged into a 'cigar lighter' socket and are suitable for powering laptop computers, telephone chargers and the like. At 350 watts, they are using 30 amps (12 volt DC), and the wiring and fuse must be capable of carrying this load.

There are many small inverters on the market, and some small, cheap inverters will not deliver their advertised power output continuously, so the sine wave may be poor.

Larger inverters, up to about 800 watts

Capable of running electric drills, blenders, small microwave ovens and the like, they really need to be permanently wired directly to their own circuit breaker and battery switch, because they draw up to 70 amps.

Using a 600 watt appliance for 10 minutes will take about 8 amp hours from your battery. Run for an hour, it will use 50 amp hours.

They should have one or two 240 volt outlets, completely separate from the mains 240 volt sockets.

Reproduced by permission of Victron Energy

Large inverters, up to about 3000 watts

At 250 amps, these are permanently wired to the battery system and supply the boat's AC 'ring main'. They must never be joined to the mains AC, so special switching is fitted to ensure automatic changeover to the mains when shore power is connected.

A 3 kW appliance will reduce a 400 amp hour battery to a 50% state of charge in around half an hour.

Some larger inverters double as mains battery chargers, so when connected to shore power, the batteries can be recharged.

AC equivalent of DC loads to size inverter

AC appliance	watts	start-up load watts	start-up current DC amps	running current DC amps	running time in 24 hr	DC amp hours in 24 hr
Blender	300	600	56	28	0.08	2
Desktop computer	300			28	2	56
Electric drill	350	600	56	32	0.08	3
Hairdryer	1000			93	0.08	7
Iron	1000			93	0.5	46
Kettle	2000			185	0.5	93
Laptop computer	50			5	2	9
Microwave oven	600			56	0.5	28
Midi Hi-Fi	100			9	4	37
Toaster	1000			93	0.08	7
TV	100			9	2	19
TV/video recorder/DVD	150			14	2	28
Vacuum cleaner	1000			93	0.08	7

Small inverters do not make huge demands on a boat's DC system. Anything more really needs a daily dose of shore power (or a generator running) to top up the batteries and is really suitable only for day use for those who must have more powerful mains appliances during day sailing.

ENGINE-DRIVEN AC SUPPLY

It's possible to have a 'mains' voltage AC alternator driven from the engine. These are of use where AC-powered equipment, such as a cooker, etc., will be used during periods of normal engine running. They are belt driven and absorb quite a lot of engine power, and the electricity from these units cannot be stored.

If you require an AC supply while underway with the engine running, fitting a mains-voltage, engine-driven alternator may be a sensible option. However, if you want AC power while the boat is moored, having to run the main engine to obtain it may be a poor option, as the engine will be running under too little load – a bad practice. A better, but more expensive, option is to use a *generating set*, where the engine power output is matched to the electrical load. Take specialist advice if you are going to have one of these.

GENERATING SETS

Generating sets comprise a diesel engine (sometimes petrol) driving an AC alternator and are often called *gensets*. They generate AC at mains voltage, either 110 V or 240 V, to supply domestic electrical equipment. They are usually supplied in a soundproof cocoon, and because on-board space is at a premium, they are often 'shoehorned' in, making access for maintenance severely restricted.

Built-in generator sets are normally powered by a diesel engine that will need to be supplied with cooling water and fuel, just like the propulsion system. They can produce an intrusive exhaust noise nuisance to other boats nearby and should not be run all night. Some harbour authorities limit their hours of use.

The boat's AC circuits will be supplied by either the shore power OR the genset. As the mains frequency may not be identical nor in phase with those of the genset, they must not be used to supply the boat's AC circuit simultaneously. Generally, this is prevented by an automatic interlocking system which ensures one is disconnected before the other is connected.

Gensets are designed to be self-monitoring and will shut themselves down automatically if a fault occurs. Failure of a genset to start may be due to a fault detected by the monitoring system or a fault in the monitoring system itself. The genset should be provided with a troubleshooting guide covering all these aspects.

The genset will normally use its own separate engine start battery, charged by a 12 volt DC alternator driven by the genset's engine.

Power output

These machines are rated not in kW but in kilo Volt Amps (kVA). The reasons need not concern us here, just think in terms of 1 kVA being equal to 1 kW. (Not strictly true, but near enough for our purpose.)

A small one will produce 2.5 kVA and larger boats may fit 10 kVA gensets. These machines take up a fair bit of room and are not cheap. If you must fit one, a 2.5 kVA machine will not supply very much AC power (several thousands of pounds is a lot of money to power just one electric kettle!) and a 4 kVA set is probably the lowest entry point.

Grounding (earthing)

The genset AC earth connection will be to the boat's AC grounding system, and thus to the shore power system if fitted. The genset's engine will probably be connected to the boat's DC earth system.

There are conflicting views on if and how the AC ground is connected to the boat's DC ground. This is sometimes done directly and sometimes via an isolator. The issues involved concern both electrical safety and electrolytic corrosion.

Professional advice should always be sought in the design and installation of a boat's genset system, which is beyond the scope of this book.

FUEL CELLS

Fuel cells bring a new technology to the marine leisure market. At the time of writing (2006), Max Power's AHD-100 is the only one on the market, and this compact unit burns methanol at the rate of 1.2 litres per kilowatt hour. The byproducts of combustion are water (non-potable) and a tiny amount of CO_2 (less than a baby would exhale in a night).

Reproduced by permission of Max Power

This fuel cell is designed to deliver a maximum of 100 amp hours per day, but actually produces electricity only on demand when connected to your battery bank, which acts as a buffer.

The use of a fuel cell can radically alter the design of your 12 volt DC power supply system, because the battery now has to be big enough only to supply demands of greater than 4 amps, the maximum output of the cell. Large battery banks could be a thing of the past!

If your total amp hour requirement per day is 120, then 100 could be supplied by the fuel cell and only 20 need come from electricity stored in the battery. However, if your daily requirement is 80 Ah, then the battery would need to temporarily supply any current in excess of 4 amps, but the fuel cell would need to generate only 80 Ah per day while keeping the battery fully charged.

Thus, the battery capacity need be only twice the daily deficit (above 100 Ah) for as many days as you want to be self-sufficient. For five days without running the engine, you would need a battery capacity of 200 Ah in the first example, rather than 1200 Ah without the fuel cell!

Advantages of fuel cells

- much reduced battery bank size and weight;

- very compact – the unit measures 150 mm × 380 mm × 260 mm and weighs 7 kg;

- very quiet – 47 dB at 1 metre;

- no installation costs or worries.

Disadvantages of fuel cells

- cost – around £3000 in 2006;

- cost of fuel – methanol costs £40 for 5 litres, which gives about 300 Ah;

- storage of flammable fuel – 5 l per 300 Ah.

RENEWABLE ENERGY

There are a number of ways that can allow a cruising yacht to be self-sufficient in its energy needs. Each is covered fully in the sections that follow.

1. Solar power
   Solar panels, otherwise known as photovoltaic panels, can convert the energy of the light falling on the panel into electrical energy. The process is not currently very efficient, the best being around 16%. The intensity of sunlight varies during the day and is dramatically reduced by the presence of shadows, from both clouds and structures. Along the south coast of the UK, the average number of hours of sunlight per day in July is about 7, but these will not all be equally bright. The panels must be kept clear of any shadows and need to be angled towards the sun.

2. Wind power
   A wind turbine can be made to drive a generator to produce electricity. In comparison with solar power, these are relatively efficient, but work only when the wind is blowing. They also need a minimum of 6 knots to start producing any electricity at all and produce only about 2 amps at 12 knots, the average wind found along the UK's south coast. They can, however, harness whatever wind is blowing for the full 24 hours each day.

   When used under way, the output is reduced considerably when running before the wind, due to the reduced apparent wind.

The turbine needs to be mounted clear of any wind eddies coming off the boat's rigging, structure and sails, and so needs to be mounted as high as possible. This also avoids decapitating the crew!

3. Towed water turbine

A water turbine can be towed and driven by the boat's forward speed though the water. Outputs as high as 8 amps can be obtained at a boat speed of 8 knots. A conventional towed turbine has to be rigged after the boat has got under way, and de-rigged prior to stopping, so is generally used only for longer passages.

Satisfying the power requirements

Unless your power requirements are modest, it's unlikely that a single source of power will satisfy your demands. As an example, on the UK's south coast, a single 60 watt solar panel could contribute up to 30 amp hours per day, a wind turbine up to 24 amp hours per day and, on an 8-hour passage at 5 knots, a towed turbine 24 amp hours per day.

Each, under ideal conditions, could run a well-insulated fridge for 24 hours, but you'll need a combination to cater for 'real' weather if you wish to be self-sufficient.

A friend with a Prout 38 cruising cat left the UK with three solar panels, a wind turbine and a towed turbine. He added a further two solar panels, but is self-sufficient on the east coast of the USA and the Caribbean and doesn't need to run his engines for battery charging.

Solar panels

Like the wind, the sun is free, and solar panels can be used to harness its energy. Unlike the wind, you don't get sun for 24 hours a day and the output must take this into account.

Maximum output will be given only when the sun is high in the sky on a cloudless day, so various areas of the world are given ratings of 'hours of average daily peak sunshine'. Remember, though, that they are just

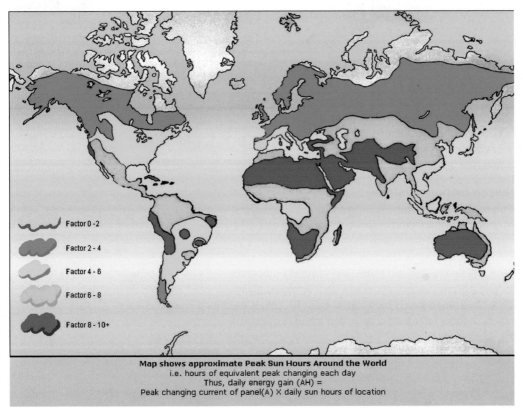

Map shows approximate Peak Sun Hours Around the World
i.e. hours of equivalent peak changing each day
Thus, daily energy gain (AH) =
Peak changing current of panel(A) X daily sun hours of location

Factor 0 - 2
Factor 2 - 4
Factor 4 - 6
Factor 6 - 8
Factor 8 - 10+

Map courtesy of BP Solar

© Crown Copyright 2000
© Crown copyright 2005, Published by the Met Office

averages. To obtain the likely 'daily output' in watt hours per day, multiply the panel's peak output by the daily sunshine figure. Dividing the watt hours per day by the system voltage will give the amp hours per day.

To maximise the output of a solar panel, it should be mounted with its surface at right angles to the sun's rays. This is difficult to arrange on a boat, which will be continually changing its direction. Also, shadows of the sails, etc. will fall on the panel, reducing its output. Ideally, the panel should be fitted on a 'steerable' mount, or even not attached to a permanent mounting but placed where it's best sited. A fully flexible panel has advantages in this respect. Several cruising sailors have reported that in the tropics there's little benefit in adjusting the angle of the panel. This is probably, because during the time of peak power the sun is high and bright anyway. I suspect they would report differently if their sailing was restricted to higher latitudes.

Types of solar panel

Development of solar panels is a continuing and important science, and we can expect further developments. There are three basic technologies:

- silicon monocrystalline;
- silicon polycrystalline;
- thin film.

© Crown copyright 2005, Published by the Met Office

Silicon monocrystalline

This is the oldest technology. Slices of a single crystal of silicon are connected in series, 36 of which give a 12 volt cell. The cost of the pure crystals is high and a large amount of energy is used in the manufacturing process. These crystals are brittle and normally mounted in a rigid frame, usually covered with toughened glass. They have the relatively high efficiency of 12–16%. One cell in shadow will cause a large reduction in output of the whole panel.

Peak power output approx. 60 watts (5 amps × 12 volts) / square metre of panel

Cost (2006) £565 / square metre of panel

Silicon polycrystalline

A modification of monocrystalline technology, with similar characteristics. These panels can be made slightly flexible to take up the curvature when fitted to the deck, and they can be walked on. The manufacturing process consumes less energy and the panels are more economic to buy per watt of output.

Peak power output approx. 110 watts (9 amps × 12 volts) / square metre of panel

Cost (2006) £950 / square metre of panel

Thin film

These use very thin layers of semiconductor laid down on a thin flexible backing, enabling very flexible but durable panels to be produced. This production process uses the fewest materials and energy, but efficiency

is only about 8%. However, because their response to various parts of the spectrum is different from the crystalline types, they give more output in the blue and green part of the spectrum. They therefore have more output in higher latitudes than is suggested by the wattage rating of the panels, especially in the winter or when overcast, where output can exceed that of the other types by as much as 30% in similar conditions.

Because of the construction, one cell in shadow will not have a large effect on the panel's output, unlike the crystalline types, which may lose up to 50% output from just the shadow of a rope.

Peak power output approx. 50 watts (4 amps × 12 volts) / square metre of panel

Cost (2006) £570 / square metre of panel

Comparing the three types of panel

During tests that I carried out for *Practical Boat Owner* magazine in the summer of 2005, I came up with some interesting results.

In determining the output of a panel, you can't necessarily rely on the rated wattage. I measured the amp hours per day output from May until September on the UK's south coast, under various cloud conditions, for rigid, semi-rigid and flexible panels, and the following charts show what you can expect, on average, throughout the summer.

The role of solar panels on a yacht

The daily output will depend on the location, season and cloud cover. Along the south coast of England in summer we may get six hours of peak sun per day, but, on the other hand, we may get close to zero. In good summer weather, output could be as high as 24 amp hours per day per square metre of panel from a thin film panel, and with the same panel on an overcast day, you could end up with 10 amp hours a day per square metre. On average it could keep a well-insulated fridge running without discharging the ship's batteries. We would need a large panel area to supply all our needs during a UK summer.

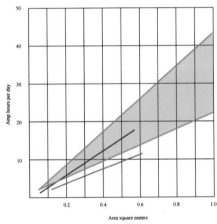

—— Flexible (good output in cloudy conditions and shadows)
—— Semi-rigid
—— Rigid panels (need direct sun)

Solar Panel Output
Based on 6 hours peak output, typical of
Equator or northern European summer

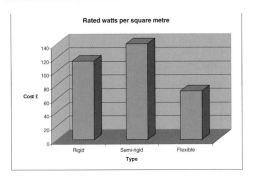

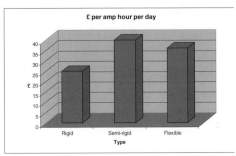

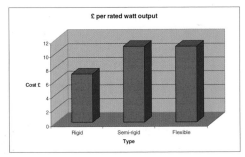

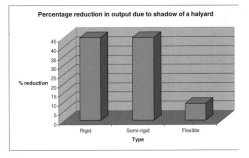

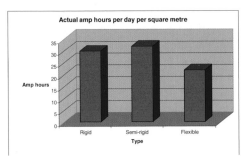

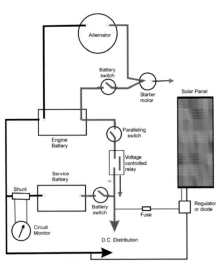

In most cases, it's unlikely that solar panels will wholly satisfy the boat's electrical demands, so other sources will be necessary. At around £570/square metre of thin film panel (2006 prices), giving a maximum of 24 amp hours per day in the UK summer, we can see the scale of the problem.

Connection

Except for the very smallest output panels, a regulator is required. Some authorities also suggest a blocking diode, as at night the panels could work in reverse

Solar Panel Circuit

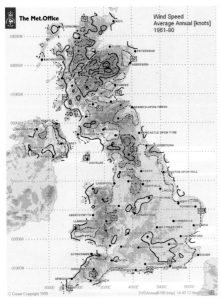

© Crown copyright, Published by the Met Office

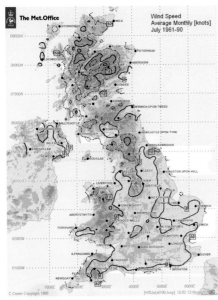

© Crown copyright, Published by the Met Office

and discharge the battery. Others dispute the need for them. TF panels incorporate blocking diodes, so external diodes are not needed in any case. Multiple panels can be controlled by a single controller/regulator but each panel needs its own diode.

Some controllers can regulate a combination of solar panels and a wind turbine.

Regulation

For trickle charging with a panel output of no more than 1 watt for each 10 amp, hours of battery capacity, no regulation is required. Greater outputs need a regulator, although 'live-aboards' may choose to switch the panels on and off as required.

Maintenance

Panels have a good life expectancy these days, with many framed panels having a 20-year guarantee. However, semi-rigid panels have only a one-year guarantee, while fully flexible TF panels are guaranteed for three years.

Maintenance is minimal. Make sure the connections are sound and the surface clean.

Wind turbines

Wind is free, so it would seem logical to harness its energy to generate electricity. However, the average windspeed may not be enough to satisfy your needs. Average annual or seasonal windspeeds can often be obtained from the Internet for the region in which you will be sailing.

Types of turbine

There are two types of turbine: those with blades like a propeller and those that look more like a vertical cylinder.

The cylinder type

These are no more than trickle chargers with outputs in milliamps rather than amps. They will maintain the charge of a battery while the boat is on its mooring, but because they won't charge a discharged battery in 15 knots of wind, the weekly output is no more than around 15 amp hours. Because of the low output, they don't require a regulator.

With no whirling blades, this type is inherently safe and noise levels are very low. They are ideal for maintaining battery charge when the boat is not being used and there's no access to mains power.

The propeller type

With diameters of up to 1.2 metres and rotation speeds up to 2000 rpm, these machines can be dangerous, so they must be mounted well out of harm's way. On ketches they are often mounted on the mizzen mast, where they are in faster and less disturbed airflow, but generally they're mounted on a pole at the stern. Some skippers restrain blades with straps to prevent rotation when their power isn't required. In this case, they must be within reach but not too low to be a hazard.

Given the right conditions, these machines can contribute significantly to the on-board electrical demands. They can, however, be noisy. The noisiest seem to be those with long slim blades and this noise 'ululates' as blade speed varies in the turbulent airflow around the boat. The noise can disturb a quiet anchorage, and this type of turbine is banned from use in some marinas.

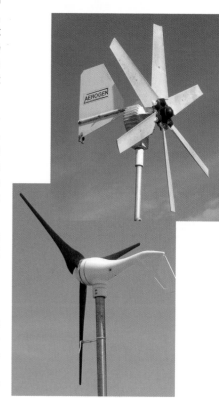

Vibration can occur with propeller-type turbines, often due to pitch differences on each blade, and this should be rectified to prevent shaking components loose.

Wind turbine output

Quoted output of a wind turbine is often the maximum that it will produce. Although output curves vary, a reasonable generalisation is a straight line output curve from zero at start-up speed to its maximum at around 30 to 40 knots. Start-up speed is around 6–8 knots for most models.

Wind speed

As an example, the summer average wind speed along the south coast of England is around 12 knots,

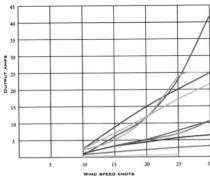

Rutland 503
Ampair Pacific 100
Aero4gen
Rutland 913
D 400
AirX
Aquair 100 wind/water
Duogen wind/water
Dolphin
Ampair Pacific 300

Wind generator outputs

Generator output	Amps at 9 knots	Amp hrs per day at 9 knots
Aero2Gen	0.3	7.2
Aero4Gen	0.8	19.2
Aero6Gen	1.6	38.4
Air X	1	24
Pacific 100	1	24
Duogen	1.5	36
D400	3.8	91.2
Rutland 503	0.4	9.6
Rutland 913	1	24

while on a trade wind passage the wind may average 25 knots. Because of the surface friction, wind speed at the height that the wind turbine will be mounted is reduced by as much as 50% and turbulence from the boat's structure and rig will reduce the turbine speed even more. Turbulence could be a factor in an anchorage as well. Anchorages chosen for their shelter can reduce the local wind speed and so inhibit the wind turbine's output.

Under way, the boat's speed will change the true wind speed, so that on a downwind passage, the apparent wind speed may be considerably reduced. Going to windward, although apparent wind speed is increased, turbulence from the mainsail will play havoc with the airflow over the turbine.

In the summer of 2005, I carried out tests on wind turbines for *Practical Boat Owner* magazine. The average wind in the summer along the UK's south coast at 3 metres above sea level is only 9 knots, and a selection of wind turbines gave the following results.

The role of the wind turbine for on-board power generation

Because of the factors outlined above, it's unlikely that a wind turbine will satisfy all of your electrical demands all of the time. At worst, in some places it's not worth fitting one at all. At best, it will almost certainly need to be supplemented by some other form of generator.

Commonly, 'live-aboards' supplement the wind turbine with solar panels, but the engine-mounted alternator can also be used. A careful analysis of your electrical demands and cruising area (and season) needs to be made to weigh up the cost and benefit of fitting a wind turbine.

With prices varying from around £300 to £1000, the wind may be free, but the cost of generation certainly isn't. Only serious users of on-board power sources with no cheaper or alternative power should consider fitting a turbine, although a cylinder type could be useful for maintenance charging the battery of a boat on a mooring.

Connecting the turbine

Output of a turbine can be high, so the output cable must be fused to protect the cable should a short circuit occur. Obviously the fuse's rating must be greater than the maximum output of the turbine, and the cable must not only be of sufficient size to carry the current, but also sufficient to reduce the voltage loss in the cable.

The output should also be regulated to prevent over-charging the batteries. Regulators can be of the *shunt type*, which dissipate the excess power as heat, or electronic *switches*, which disconnect the turbine from the battery once the battery is charged.

Regulators are available to charge multiple banks of batteries and also to combine solar, wind and engine generators. These specialist regulators should be spec-ified as part of the overall electrical generating system.

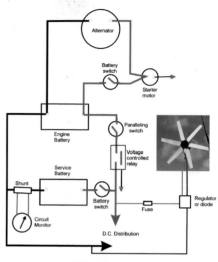

Wind Generator Circuit

Maintenance

Generally, wind turbines require no maintenance, although it's prudent to inspect the tightness of connec-tions from time to time, especially if there's any vibra-tion. After several seasons' continuous use, there may be a need to replace the carbon brushes that pick up the current. Securing the blades against rotation when turbine output isn't required will prolong the life of the brushes. Some turbines have no commutator brushes on the generator, but they still need brushes on the slip rings that allow the turbine to align itself to the wind.

Always ensure that you turn the turbine out of the wind to stop rotation and then secure the blades to prevent their turning before you start any work.

Water turbines

A propeller-shaped turbine connected by a rope to a boat-mounted generator can be towed behind the boat. Equally, a turbine/generator unit can be mounted on a leg immersed in the water.

With the boat under way, electricity is generated due to the forward motion of the boat. The drag produced

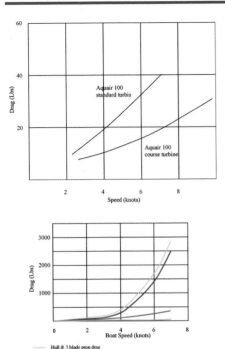

Hull & 3 blade prop drag
Hull drag
3 blade prop drag
Towed turbine drag

Comparison of towed turbine drag

by the towed turbine gives a slight reduction in boat speed, but users do not see this as a disadvantage. If the boat travels faster than the turbine's maximum design speed, the rotor will surface. Course pitch rotors are available for higher speed, and in marginal cases, heavier rope or a sinker weight can be used. The boat needs to be sailing at a minimum of around 3 knots before the turbine can be used.

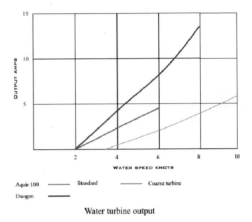

| Aquir 100 | ——— | Standard | ——— | Coarse turbine |
| Duogen | ——— | | | |

Water turbine output

Continuous steady output of the towed turbine in amps is around half the boat speed in knots. So, cruising downwind at 6 knots one can reliably expect a daily output of over 70 amp hours. This can come close to fulfilling the boat's electrical needs.

The DuoGen, new to the market, has the water turbine mounted on the end of a counterbalanced arm that is lowered into the water.

Often, the generator can also be modified quickly to be driven by a wind turbine, so owners of this system can use it as a wind turbine at anchor or on short passages, but re-rig it as a towed turbine for long passages.

Removable propeller blades can be fitted to the Duo-Gen turbine, which is then mounted vertically to convert it into a wind turbine.

Courtesy of Electric Energy, Ltd

67

Connection

Electrical connection and requirements are the same as for a wind turbine.

Maintenance

No special maintenance procedures are required, other than those appropriate to a wind turbine, but a spare towed rotor needs to be carried to allow for accidental loss.

Rotor diameter 1.1m

Turning circle 260mm radius

Switches and Relays

SWITCHES

A switch allows a circuit to be 'made' or 'broken' so that a light, motor or whatever can be activated or isolated.

A switch has at least one pair of contacts that can be made or broken, but can be much more complicated. It can make or break several circuits at a time, or can be made to switch between one or more circuits, either individually or in unison.

- Single pole, single throw (SPST), i.e. ON/OFF.

- Double pole, single throw (DPST), i.e. ON/OFF for two different circuits at the same time.

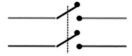

- Single pole, double throw (SPDT), i.e. switches between two different circuits.

- Double pole, double throw (DPDT), i.e. switches between two different circuits for two circuits at the same time.

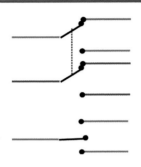

Another variation is that double throw switches may have a centre 'OFF' position so that you may choose between OFF and either one or another circuit:

Obviously the DPDT switch may also be found with a centre OFF position.

You don't have to use all the terminals, so you can tailor the switch to suit your circuit.

Switches may have solder terminals or 'spade' terminals, the latter being easier to install in boat circuits as you can use crimp terminals to fit the wires.

Troubleshooting switches

You can check the operation of a switch using a multimeter – with the switch 'open' the resistance should be infinite and with the switch 'closed' the resistance should be zero.

The more wire terminals there are on the switch, the more you have to think about which terminal does what. It's sometimes easier to draw a 'mini circuit' to see what's happening. Where there are only two, that's easy. With more it gets complicated.

- When you move the switch lever (or rocker), the terminals in use are usually opposite to the direction of movement – if in doubt check with the multimeter.

Active contacts

- Double pole switches have their 'paired' contacts on the same side (in the plane of movement of the switch).

RELAYS

Relays do the same job as switches. Instead of the switch being operated manually, a current passes through a coil of wire, which then becomes an electromagnet. When the electromagnet is energised, it moves a soft iron core inside the coil. The movement of this core operates contactors so that a current can flow through the circuit.

Coil

Soft iron
core
inside

Contactor
lever

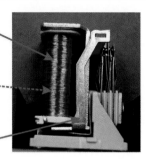

Two sets of contacts

Usually, only a very small current flows through the coil, while the contactors can handle a much higher one. All the time the relay is energised, it is drawing some power from the boat's electrical system – generally a tenth of an amp or so, but it can be a lot more for larger relays.

Sometimes it's better to connect a normal switch and run a thinner wire, where it's a long length, and then use a relay to switch a heavy current on and off.

Like switches, the terminals may be of the soldered type or spades. Spade terminals are best suited for use on boats as you can use crimped terminals for your connections.

Relay contacts may be 'normally open', i.e. they close when energised, or 'normally closed', so that they open when energised. You may even find a combination of both on the same relay.

Where part of an engine-start system, these relays may be mounted on a base socket. You may find spares in an auto-accessory shop.

Automotive-type relays often have their terminal configuration marked on the side of the plastic casing. If not, you'll need to use a multimeter to check which terminal is which.

- The coil terminals will have a resistance of several hundred ohms or more.

- The contacts will have either zero resistance (closed) or infinite resistance (open).

Troubleshooting relays

- Check the coil resistance with a multimeter, if it's infinity, then the coil is faulty.

- Apply 12 volts to the coil terminals – you should hear a click.

- Measure the resistance across the contact terminals with a multimeter. The open (infinite resistance) ones should close and have zero resistance, as the contacts change over when the coil is energised.

Connections

CONNECTIONS

Connections are the heart of the electrical system and if we are not meticulous in making them, they can be its downfall.

- They must be secure.

- They must be supported so that the wiring is not taking any load which might make it liable to being pulled out.

- They must be protected from corrosion.

- They must be accessible.

- They should be identifiable.

- The strongest permanent joint, having the least electrical resistance, is a soldered joint made on new, bright wire. However, a soldered joint may melt in the event of a short circuit.

Corrosion is the enemy of all cable joints on a boat. Any exposed cable joint should be protected using silicone grease.

The connection may be a joint between just two wires or a joint between multiple wires. There are a number of different ways to make the joints and you need to consider if the joint is to be permanent or if it needs to be undone from time to time.

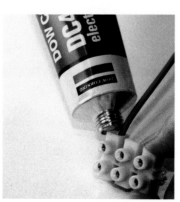

Signal wires are small in diameter because they carry a very small current. They are typically used for instrument wiring and are fairly fragile, thus they need special consideration when being joined.

There are two schools of thought on whether the end of a wire should be 'tinned' with solder or not (see chapter 'Soldering').

- Soldered joints use a *flux* to remove oxidisation from the surfaces to be joined. This flux may be acidic and can cause subsequent weakening of the wire.

- On small-diameter, multi-strand wire, stresses can be induced by movement at the junction of the soldered wire and the unsoldered wire.

- The screw of a screw terminal and the crimping process are both unable to 'squash' the soldered part of the cable and joints may be less secure.

Most technicians recommend that the ends of the wires should not be soldered.

Terminal blocks

These allow joints to be made and remade as required.

- Remove just sufficient insulation to fit into the terminal using a wire stripper.

- Insert the wire into the terminal and tighten the clamping screw, ensuring that the screw presses down on the centre of the wire's core.

'Chocolate box' connectors are *not* ideal for use on a boat. If used, seal the joints with silicone grease to prevent corrosion of the cable.

Connector blocks should be made from marine-grade materials, which rules out those bought from the local car shop. If they are to be used with small-diameter signal wires, such as those used for instrument connections, they should have a clamping leaf to hold the wire, otherwise the wire's strands may be broken as you tighten the securing screw.

Marine-grade 'bus bar' connectors should be used with crimped terminals, preferably self-sealing ones.

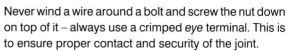

Never wind a wire around a bolt and screw the nut down on top of it – always use a crimped *eye* terminal. This is to ensure proper contact and security of the joint.

Splices

Splices are permanent connections between one or more cables. They can be made using crimped splices or the joint can be soldered.

If you crimp, it's best to use heat-shrinkable, self-adhesive cable splices.

- Remove just sufficient insulation from the end of the wire so that the wire will go into the terminal AND the insulation will be covered by the terminal's own insulation – this ensures that no bare wire is visible.

- Insert one wire into the terminal.

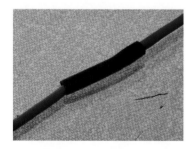

- Use a crimping tool on the part of the joint containing the wire, squeeze it *very tightly* to crimp the terminal onto the wire.

- Insert the other stripped wire into the other end of the terminal and repeat the crimping procedure.

- Use of the correct force and the correct size of terminal for the wire will result in a secure joint.

- If you can pull the wires out easily, you'll need to remake the joint properly.

If you solder, cover the joint with heat-shrinkable, self-adhesive sleeving. Soldering has its own dedicated chapter.

CRIMPED CONNECTIONS

'Spade' and 'Bullet'-type terminals

These can be undone and remade as required. As with the crimped splice, the end of the wire is stripped, the wire inserted into the connector and crimped tight using a crimping tool. It's best to use heat-shrinkable, self-adhesive cable terminals.

Crimped connectors come in a variety of shapes and three different colour-coded sizes. Using an oversized connector will make a weak joint.

Crimping tools and connectors are available cheaply from car shops. The connectors are probably made of steel and the crimping tool will not allow sufficient pressure to be applied. They don't make very strong joints and wires are easy to pull out of the crimped joints.

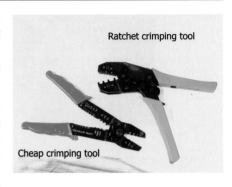

Ratchet crimping tool

Cheap crimping tool

Ideally, use a ratchet crimping tool, which, although more expensive, will make a secure joint. This robust tool exerts sufficient force to make a proper joint on any size wire that it's designed for. You use a repeated squeezing action and continue until the tool automatically releases at the correct pressure. It has three *anvils*, each of a different size. Each anvil is colour-coded – red being for the smallest crimp, blue a mid-sized one and yellow the largest.

The anvils are matched to colour-coded crimp connectors, each of a different size and designed for different-sized wires, NOT the colour of the insulation! You use the red anvil for red connectors, etc.

Wire	Red	Blue	Yellow
mm²	0.25–1.65	1.04–2.63	2.63–6.64
AWG	22–18	16–14	12–10

Making a crimp connection

- Strip insulation from the end of the wire.

- The stripper jaws have four notches suitable for different wire core sizes.

- Insert the wire into the most suitably sized of the four 'V' notches.

- Squeeze and release the handles to strip the wire.

- Insert the bared wire into the connector.

- Squeeze the connector with the crimping tool to clamp the connector to the wire. Crimp connectors are colour-coded according to wire size – use the same colour crimp tool aperture as the connector and the correct colour for the wire gauge. If the wire is too small, double it over to make it thicker.

- Apply silicone grease to seal the terminal if required.

Making a heavy-duty crimp connection

- Cut the cable to length.

- Remove just sufficient insulation using a hobby knife …

● ... so that the bared wire is the same length as the terminal's collar.

● Take the heavy-duty crimping tool.

● Place the terminal in the correct sized hole for the gauge of the terminal and cable.

● Place the crimper into the vice and push the cable into the terminal ...

● ... until it is fully inserted with no bare wire showing.

● Close the vice ...

- … until the ends of the crimper in the jaws of the vice make hard contact.

- Place a cut length of adhesive heat-shrink tubing over the joint.

- Heat the heat-shrink with a hot air gun until it has shrunk and made a tight fit over the joint.

- The finished joint with a little adhesive visible at each end of the tubing.

SIGNAL WIRE CONNECTORS

These make a permanent joint between two or three small-diameter signal wires. Use 'Eton 23' or 'Scotchlok' type connectors that are gel-filled and seal automatically when the joint is made.

Signal wire connectors are not readily attainable unless you go to a specialist supplier, where they are available only by the 100. They have the advantage that they are designed specially for small-diameter signal wire, such as that used for instrument connections, and are light enough not to need direct support.

Making a signal wire connection

- Don't strip the wires.

- Insert the wires into the connector.

- Squeeze the top and bottom of the connector with a pair of pliers. The connector will pierce the insulation to make a good connection and seal the joint automatically with grease.

HEAT-SHRINKING

- Heat-shrink tubing is put over the joint.

- Heat is then applied using an electric hot air gun (a paint stripper – a hairdryer is too cool), which shrinks the tube to grip the wire and joint tightly.

- Some heat-shrink tubing is coated internally with adhesive, which melts when heated. This makes a very corrosion-proof joint.

INSULATING AWKWARD JOINTS

Where it's difficult to apply conventional insulation, such as a sleeve, liquid insulation is a very convenient alternative. This is painted on and the required thickness is built up in layers. This is very convenient on the connections at the back of small plugs and sockets.

CONNECTIONS AT THE BASE OF THE MAST

To allow a mast to be un-stepped, cables running down it must have connectors at its base. These connectors are often a cause of problems due to corrosion, but there are ways of minimising this.

Waterproof deck plugs and sockets

These are available in a number of different forms. The plug and socket have a waterproof joint, which, in time, may allow water to enter the pins and cables. Annual cleaning of the contacts is a good idea, as is some form of physical protection from damage to the cables.

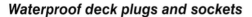

Waterproof through-deck glands

An alternative to a deck plug is to lead the cables through the deck, using waterproof deck glands. The connections are then made inside the boat using some form of terminal. This method keeps the connections in a far less corrosive atmosphere.

Swan neck deck pipe

In this set-up, a curved large-diameter pipe passes through the deck. All the cables are run through the pipe so that connections may be made inside the cabin. While not absolutely waterproof, only large quantities of 'green water' passing over the foredeck will allow any to leak below. The advantage is that it is very easy to thread the cables through the deck, and nothing needs to be undone.

Keel-stepped masts

No deck joints are needed for keel-stepped masts, as the cables exit the mast below the deck.

Wiring

Electrical wire used on boats should be tinned along its whole length. This is expensive, so most production boats have 'automotive-type' wire, which allows corrosion to spread along the strands of wire under the insulation. This makes it impossible to remake joints successfully. Where one end of a wire is located in a damp atmosphere, tinned wire should always be used.

Do not run wires through the bilge where their condition will deteriorate.

Use a push wiring threader to run wires through difficult places.

1. Insert one end into the conduit or gap through which you need to run the wire.

2. Then push the threader through.

3. Use the threader to pull the electric wire all the way through.

Some alloy masts have internal conduits, provided to carry wiring running up the mast. Wires dropped through the main section of the mast will slap and chafe. A push threader can be used to run mouse lines and cables up the mast's conduit.

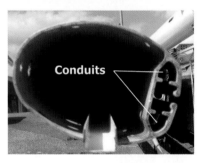

Conduits

I have pushed a threader successfully all the way up the conduit in a 15-metre mast.

TIPS

1. Run a mouse line in case you need to run another cable later. The mouse line can be run through the conduit (or other routes where a cable is run) at the same time as you install a cable with the threader. The mouse line is then left in place for the next time

you need it. The mouse line should be twice as long as its route, so that you don't pull it all the way through when you use it.

2. Use grommets to protect the insulation where you run wires through bulkheads, etc.

3. Support cable runs regularly along their length.

4. Cable should not come under strain, which could cause connections to be pulled apart.

5. A very neat and secure way to protect and support cables is to run them in a corrugated trunking. If cables are already in place, split trunking is available that can be placed around the cables in situ.

6. If you need to run cables to terminals from the trunking, use 'Beta duct' trunking, which has holes and slots.

7. Make a wiring diagram of any new work.

HEAVY-DUTY CIRCUITS

A DC electric motor will overheat and suffer early failure if the supply voltage is reduced. Motors with high current requirements need special care with their wiring circuits to maintain an adequate voltage. Normally, a voltage drop of 10% is the maximum allowed.

The operating switch will not handle the required current, so a relay is introduced into the circuit. A relay consists of an electromagnet that can be operated by the low current; its contactors then carry the high current required to operate the motor, or whatever.

This keeps the switching current low, but heavy-duty contacts handle the high current load of the motor. Proper siting of the relay will keep the length of the high-current circuit to a minimum.

Starter motors and sheet winches

These are operated with the engine stopped.

Starter motors normally run for a very short time and have a relatively short run of very heavy cable. Provided connections are clean and well made, they make only small demands on a dedicated engine start battery.

Sheet winches may have relatively long cable runs and the demands on the battery system can be significant, so that voltage drop at the motor needs to be minimised. Adhere strictly to the manufacturer's wiring requirements.

Bow thrusters and anchor windlasses

To keep voltage drop to a minimum, these are normally used with the engine running to prolong the life of their electric motors and to minimise battery drain. These units can't be powered directly from the engine alternator, as it won't produce enough current.

There are two schools of thought on powering these machines:

1. Use the domestic battery

   Long, very heavy and expensive cables run from the domestic battery bank. As these cables may carry up to 300 amps and may have a circuit length of 20 metres, a cross-sectional area of 200 mm^2 may be needed. That's a diameter of 16 mm! This is for a windlass with a 2000 lb pull. A more typical 1000 watt windlass will still need a cable of around 10 mm diameter.

2. Use a separate battery mounted close to the demand

   The heavy cable length is kept to a minimum by placing a dedicated battery close to the windlass or bow thruster. This is charged by a smaller cable from the engine. The charging cable needs to be rated to carry the maximum charging current only. The lower

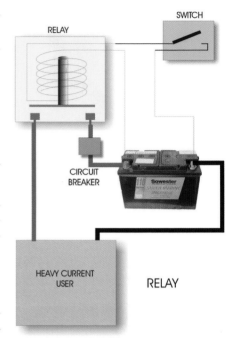

RELAY

cost of the lighter cable may outweigh the cost of the extra battery. The disadvantage of this method is the weight of this battery forward in the boat.

WIRE CURRENT RATINGS

A wire must be capable of carrying the maximum current in the circuit. All wires have a *current rating*. A 5 amp wire must carry no more than 5 amps. Note that wires bundled together can carry less current because they will heat up.

Wiring for sensitive equipment should not allow more than a 3% voltage drop. Normally this is more restrictive than the current rating because it depends on the length (both positive and negative) of the wires.

Other wiring may be allowed a 10% voltage drop along its total length.

Wire sizes required for a given length of cable run (Length is the sum of the positive and negative wires)

Wire size 3% voltage drop (Critical applications – bilge pumps, nav. lights, electronics, etc.)

LENGTH	CURRENT (amps)								
	5 a	10 a	15 a	20 a	25 a	30 a	40 a	50 a	100 a
5 m	16	12	10	10	8	8	6	6	2
10 m	12	10	8	6	6	4	4	2	1/0
20 m	10	6	6	4	2	2	1	1/0	4/0
30 m	8	4	4	2	1	1/0	2/0	3/0	
40 m	6	4	2	1	1/0	2/0	3/0	4/0	
50 m	6	2	1	1/0	2/0	3/0	4/0		

Wire size 10% voltage drop (Non-critical applications – windlasses, cabin lights, etc.)

LENGTH	CURRENT (amps)								
	5 a	10 a	15 a	20 a	25 a	30 a	40 a	50 a	100 a
5 m	18	18	16	16	14	14	12	12	6
10 m	18	16	14	12	10	10	8	8	4
20 m	16	12	10	8	8	8	6	4	2
30 m	14	10	8	8	6	6	4	4	1
40 m	12	8	8	6	4	4	2	2	2/0
50 m	10	8	6	4	4	2	2	1	3/0

continued overleaf

American wire gauge 'boat cable'

AWG	18	16	14	12	10	8	6	4	2	1	1/0	2/0	3/0	4/0
mm²	0.8	1	2	3	5	8	13	19	32	40	50	62	81	103
Max. amps	20	25	35	45	60	80	120	160	210	245	285	330	385	445

Reduce current by 15% when run in engine compartment.
Standard UK wire sizes – 1, 1.5, 2.5, 4, 6, 25 and 40 mm².

INSTALLING NEW EQUIPMENT

1. Check the wire size required, according to its length and the current it has to carry, from the table above.

2. Decide if you will need to power the equipment from the battery (e.g. a VHF radio) or the panel (e.g. a new GPS).

3. Run a new positive wire from the C/B panel or the battery to a new bus bar.

4. Run a new positive wire from the bus bar to a fuse holder (or circuit breaker).

5. Run a new positive wire from the new fuse holder to the new equipment.

6. Fit an appropriately sized fuse, as recommended by the equipment manufacturer.

7. Run a new negative wire from the existing negative bus bar or a new one as appropriate.

Note:

• If you have an ammeter, its shunt should be fitted in the negative battery cable.

• Equipment supplied direct from the battery MUST have the negative cable connected via the shunt and NOT taken direct to the battery's negative terminal.

Circuit protection

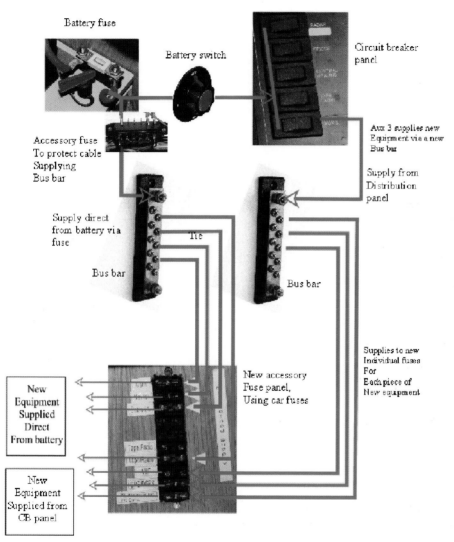

Battery fuse

Battery switch

Circuit breaker
panel

Accessory fuse
To protect cable
Supplying
Bus bar

Aux 3 supplies new
Equipment via a new
Bus bar

Supply from
Distribution
panel

Supply direct
from battery via
fuse

Tie

Bus bar

Bus bar

Supplies to new
Individual fuses
For
Each piece of
New equipment

New accessory
Fuse panel,
Using car fuses

New
Equipment
Supplied
Direct
From battery

New
Equipment
Supplied from
CB panel

NEW PROTECTED WIRING INSTALLATION

Circuits

DC CIRCUIT MONITORING

With any form of boat electrical system beyond the very basic, it's essential to monitor the flow of electricity to and from the boat's circuits, unless shore power is going to be available every night to keep the batteries fully charged.

System voltage

The voltage indicated by the voltmeter indicates whether the system is running from the batteries or is being charged.

System current

The current flow indicates the electrical demand being placed on the system.

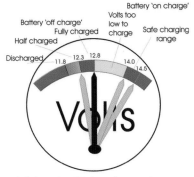

Half charged and full charge figures apply to a battery at rest, which a dedicated 'engine start' battery would be when the engine isn't running.

Used in conjunction with the voltmeter, a simple table can indicate the state of charge of the batteries.

BATTERY STATE OF CHARGE	BATTERY VOLTS			
	RESTED	0 AMPS	5 AMPS	10 AMPS
100%	12.8	12.5	12.4	12.2
90%	12.7	12.4	12.3	12.1
80%	12.6	12.3	12.2	12.0
70%	12.5	12.2	12.1	11.9
60%	12.4	12.1	12.0	11.8
50%	12.3	12.0	11.9	11.7
40%	12.2	11.9	11.8	11.6
30%	12.1	11.8	11.7	11.5
20%	12.0	11.7	11.6	
10%	11.9	11.6		
FLAT	11.8	11.5		

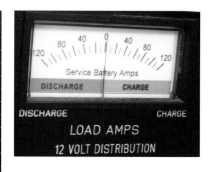

Suitably placed, an ammeter can measure the current entering or leaving the battery.

Battery state of charge

A sophisticated meter can measure the current entering or leaving the battery, indicate its state of charge and also how long the battery will last if the current drain continues at that rate.

How it's done

A special, very accurately calibrated resistor, called a *shunt*, is inserted into the negative cable of the system. The ammeter measures how much the voltage drops along the shunt and is thus able to deduce the current flowing through it using 'Ohm's Law'. The voltmeter measures the voltage between the resistor and the positive side of the circuit. The size of the shunt is determined by the maximum current flow in the circuit.

Because some items of equipment, such as the VHF or gas detector, may be supplied directly from the battery, fitting the shunt in the positive line will miss some of the current flow. Therefore, the shunt should always be inserted in the negative cable.

The shunt must be installed in the negative line close to the battery that it is monitoring, so that it measures ALL the current flowing in or out of that battery, including those items 'hot-wired' to the battery.

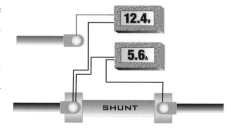

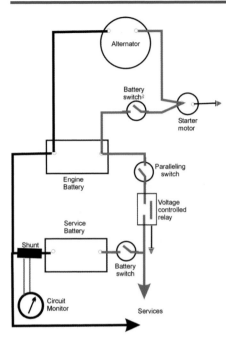

Circuit monitoring

CIRCUIT PROTECTION
Low-voltage DC circuits

If, for some reason, a live (known as the *hot* wire in the USA) DC positive wire is allowed to touch a DC negative wire, a large current will flow, because essentially there will be little resistance to current flow. This is known as a short circuit, because the current takes the shortest path back to the battery and thus bypasses the rest of the circuit. As a result, the wires carrying the excessive current will heat up, which, in turn, heats the wire's insulation and a fire may result.

A device must be introduced into the circuit to protect against an unusually high current. This will break the circuit if, for any reason, the current rises above that which the wire can carry safely.

The safety device may be a fusible link (a fuse), which has the capacity to carry very little more current than the wire can carry safely. The fuse will be destroyed if this current is exceeded, and will need to be replaced with another of the same value to restore the circuit. Keep spare fuses of all required ratings in case a fuse blows. Some fuses are *slow-blow* (anti-surge), in that they will not fail until an excessive current flows for some seconds, to allow for transient surges; others are *fast-blow*, which fail immediately an excessive current flows. Always replace like with like.

Alternatively, a circuit breaker can be installed in the circuit to break the circuit in the advent of an excessive current. Circuit breakers sense the rise in current either thermally or magnetically and *trip* to prevent an excessive current. They can be reset to restore the circuit. Some circuit breakers may incorporate an 'ON/OFF' switch. Others are not designed to act as a normal switch and these must be provided with a separate switch to activate the circuit.

When a fuse blows or a circuit breaker trips, it is normal to allow the circuit to be restored *once* only, before troubleshooting is carried out. This is because any small surge produced within the circuit could cause a sensitive breaker to trip or a fast-blow fuse to fail, even though no short is present. In the event of a recurrence, the cause must be found.

A fuse or circuit breaker in a wiring circuit protects only the wiring and not any component within the circuit.

Expert's tip

A fuse has an electrical resistance and, if used inappropriately, may cause a malfunction of a component. For instance, consider a central heating unit. This has a high start-up current and incorporates a circuit that shuts it down if the supply voltage drops below a critical value. If the heater supply cable has a high voltage drop and you protect the cable with a fuse rather than a circuit breaker, the heater may not start unless the battery is fully charged, because of the additional voltage drop across the fuse.

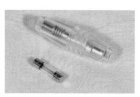

Inline fuse holder with glass fuse

Circuit breakers have little resistance and would not cause the above problem.

Short circuits

These allow very high currents to flow (a DC circuit could allow 800 amps) and can result in an electrical fire.

Panel fuse holder with galass fuse

Short circuits can be caused by a breakdown in insulation by chafing, ultraviolet light or contamination. They can also be caused when a wire becomes loose and detached from a terminal due to incorrect making of the joint or the joint coming under strain. This could allow the free end of the wire to touch another of opposite polarity.

Automotive fuse

Fuses and circuit breakers

Equipment often has an internal fuse for self-protection. It's usually of a low value. Wiring supplying the equipment needs to be protected by a fuse or circuit breaker in case of a short circuit. The amperage rating of the fuse or circuit breaker must *never* exceed the current rating of the wire.

Heavy duty fuse

All distribution wires must be protected, including the battery, where there's a chance of positive and nega-

tive wires coming into contact – note, an equipment case may be connected to negative.

Multiple circuits are protected by only one fuse or breaker and this must be rated for the lowest rated wire.

Battery fuses mounted in the battery compartment should ideally be of the non-arcing variety, because of the risk of explosion from a gassing battery.

Pros and cons

Circuit breakers:

- are relatively expensive;
- can be reset;
- can also act as circuit switches in some cases.

Fuses:

- are cheap (as are fuse holders);
- may be inserted 'in-line' when you add an extra component;
- need to be replaced if they blow, meaning spares are required;
- 'age' with continued use and may blow under normal current conditions.

Siting of fuses/circuit breakers

Most, if not all, fuses and circuit breakers will be placed in full view on the DC distribution panel by the builder.

Subsequent additions, including those made by the supplier, often incorporate 'in-line' fuses that are hidden away, with their presence often unknown to the boat's owner. This practice is common, even among professional installers, and is to be deplored. If in-line fuses are to be used, their existence and location should be noted on the wiring diagram.

There will sometimes be a couple of spare circuit breakers on the panel, which may be used for additional circuits if they are of the correct rating.

If you run out of breakers, then you really should fit an auxiliary fuse or circuit breaker panel, or at least a fuse-box in a known and accessible place.

Mains AC circuits

The reason for AC circuit protection is identical to the DC circuit, i.e. to protect the wiring in order to prevent fire. Additionally, there needs to be a different type of circuit breaker, which detects any minute flow of current to earth, to protect human life.

The distribution panel will have circuit breakers protecting individual circuits and should incorporate a special circuit breaker known as a *residual current device* (RCD) or *earth leakage circuit breaker* (ELCB) or *residual current circuit breaker* (RCCB). This will trip out for a very small current (0.03 amps–30 mA, or so) flowing to earth caused by an earth leak. A more detailed discussion of this topic is given in the chapter 'Electrical Supply'.

In the UK, the wiring of items plugged into AC sockets (outlets), is protected by a fused plug. This fuse should never have a rating greater than that of the appliance's mains cable.

FAULTS IN AN ELECTRIC CIRCUIT

Finding a fault in an electrical circuit entails a methodical approach, but luck can play its part.

Flow process of checking a faulty electrical circuit

If several pieces of equipment are protected by one circuit breaker or fuse:

- Check others on the same circuit by switching them on.

- Check, by observation, that the circuit breaker has not tripped or the fuse blown – remove the fuse and measure its resistance.

- Check the supply to the circuit breaker/fuse – if there's an associated indicator light, its illumination confirms a supply.

- Fuse contacts can become corroded, check that they are clean by removing the fuse and cleaning it if necessary.

If there's shared wiring for part of the circuit:

- Check other items on the shared circuit by switching them on.

If only one item is affected:

1. If it's a light:

   - Check the bulb with a multimeter.

   - Check the voltage in the bulb holder.

   - Check for corrosion of the contacts by removing the bulb.

2. If it's electronic and remains dead:

   - Check that the power supply is plugged in properly.

   - Check the voltage supply at the plug with a multimeter.

   - Check the internal fuse by removing it and measuring its resistance – this may involve opening the case.

If there are connections along the circuit's wiring, especially in damp areas or at deck plugs:

- Check these connections carefully.

- Check for corrosion visually.

- Check the supply voltage with a multimeter.

If the equipment is difficult to reach, such as a masthead navigation light:

- Check continuity of the circuit where it's easiest first, using a multimeter.

- Check, using a multimeter, the supply voltage at the deck plug or where the circuit is broken to allow the mast to be un-stepped.

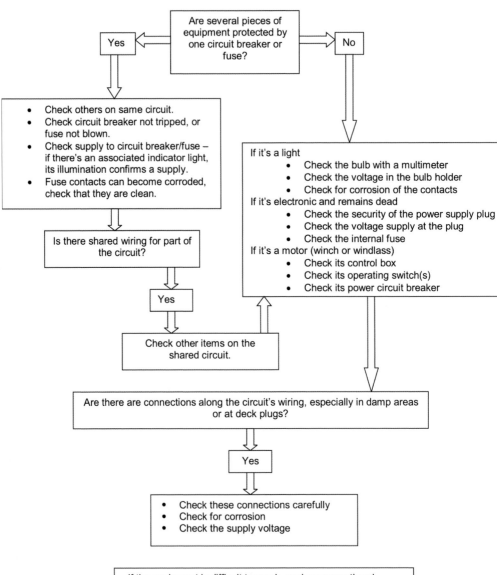

Are several pieces of equipment protected by one circuit breaker or fuse?

Yes

No

- Check others on same circuit.
- Check circuit breaker not tripped, or fuse not blown.
- Check supply to circuit breaker/fuse – if there's an associated indicator light, its illumination confirms a supply.
- Fuse contacts can become corroded, check that they are clean.

If it's a light
- Check the bulb with a multimeter
- Check the voltage in the bulb holder
- Check for corrosion of the contacts

If it's electronic and remains dead
- Check the security of the power supply plug
- Check the voltage supply at the plug
- Check the internal fuse

If it's a motor (winch or windlass)
- Check its control box
- Check its operating switch(s)
- Check its power circuit breaker

Is there shared wiring for part of the circuit?

Yes

Check other items on the shared circuit.

Are there are connections along the circuit's wiring, especially in damp areas or at deck plugs?

Yes

- Check these connections carefully
- Check for corrosion
- Check the supply voltage

If the equipment is difficult to reach, such as a masthead navigation light.
- Check continuity of the circuit where it's easiest first.
- Check the supply voltage at the deck plug or where the circuit is broken to allow the mast to be un-stepped.

Finding a fault in a wiring circuit

First check the fuse or circuit breaker as above. This may not be as obvious as it would at first seem. Panel-mounted circuit breakers are no problem.

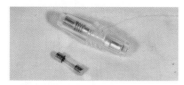

Often, though, individual components are fused with an in-line fuse in some out-of-the-way place.

This is a short-sighted policy, often done to save time. All additional fuses should be grouped together and should ideally be panel-mounted.

Some instruments have a 'built-in' fuse to protect them, but these rarely cause a problem. They are generally there to protect against connections with reversed polarity.

Lights

If a light fails to work, the bulb has probably failed or its contacts have become corroded, so check the bulb.

If the bulb is at the masthead, then some continuity checks will be worthwhile before going up the mast.

There are two ways to check circuit continuity:

1. Check the wire's resistance between two points. This may entail the use of a long extension wire for one of the probes – make sure it's of large enough cross-section to give minimal resistance.

   • Very high resistance indicates a break or poor joint.

   • Very low or zero resistance indicates no breaks.

2. Check the voltage between the positive and negative wires at points along the circuit using a multimeter. This will check both positive and negative (ground) wires in combination – it will not tell you which one has the problem, so you will then have to check the continuity of each wire separately, again using the multimeter.

   • The voltage at the far end of the circuit should be no less than 90% of the nominal voltage.

- Zero volts indicates a break in a wire.

- A large voltage drop indicates poor contacts or wire that is too small in diameter for the current it is carrying.

Wires that are run up the mast usually have a plug and socket joint at the deck, or have a connection inside the cabin, just below the mast. Deck joints are always vulnerable to corrosion, but interior joints can also be affected. These joints will always be the first port of call when something up the mast is not working but the other lights in the same circuit are functioning.

- If there's no voltage at the deck joint, the fault is between the switch panel and here.

- If there is normal voltage, then the problem is in the plug or up the mast.

Deck lights

Deck lights that have no lens are a particular problem. They have small halogen bulbs, which use little power relative to their light output, but get hot. It's for this reason that they have no lens, but it does make them susceptible to corrosion.

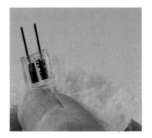

The two probe-like contacts will need to be cleaned and probably so will the socket.

Don't hold the glass bulb directly in your fingers – use a cloth or tissue – as grease from the hand will shorten the life of the bulb. Clean the bulb contacts with fine emery paper and the sockets with a very small twist drill bit. Because you may remove any protective plating in this process, the requirement for cleaning will become more frequent!

Pulpit-mounted navigation lights

These are particularly susceptible to corrosion, as they will sometimes be immersed as the bow ploughs into a wave. Ensuring that all the seals are as watertight as possible, using Vaseline or silicone grease, will help to keep corrosion at bay.

Check the lenses, visually, for condensation regularly and dry the inside as necessary.

Troubleshooting

Alternator not charging – generator warning light 'ON'

- Check the battery voltage. If the voltage is above 13.2 volts, it's probable that the bulb has failed.

- Stop the engine and check the alternator drive belt to see if it's too slack or broken.

- Start the engine.

- Increase engine revs to about half speed.

- You should see the voltage rise. The actual voltage will vary according to the battery state of charge.

- Unless the battery is heavily discharged, the voltage should always be above 13.2 volts.

- If you have an ammeter that shows the alternator output, a positive reading indicates that the alternator is charging, but the actual reading will vary according to the battery's state of charge.

- If the battery is being charged, the fault is in the warning light circuit.

- If the battery is not being charged, stop the engine and visually check all the alternator connections.

Battery not holding its charge

A battery will self-discharge over a period of time and wet cell batteries should be charged every month.

A 12 volt battery is made up of six cells, each giving a nominal 2 volts. If one cell is faulty, the other five cells will be discharged, trying to hold up the faulty cell. The battery will self-discharge rapidly and will never reach full charge. This is inevitable over time and the more deeply a battery is discharged on a regular basis, the sooner this will occur.

If you have more than one battery, it may not be obvious which one is at fault.

- Charge all batteries fully.

- Disconnect all but one battery from your system and then use this to try and start the engine.

- Ensure the battery and starter motor terminals are clean and tight.

- On a sailing boat, turn off the cooling water sea-cock to prevent flooding the engine with water.

- Operate the mechanical stop control to prevent the engine starting. If the engine is stopped electrically, apply 12 volts to the stop solenoid.

- Operate the starter for 15 seconds and observe the voltmeter.

- The battery voltage should remain above 9 volts under the load of the starter motor.

- Low volts or the starter slowing down indicate a faulty battery.

- Check each battery in turn by using the battery switches to isolate all except the battery under test.

Engine starter motor not turning

Because the starter motor's current draw is so high, the starter button or key is not connected directly to the starter motor. Instead, a starter solenoid and often a starter relay are used to limit the current to much lower values in the starter circuit. This means there are several components that can fail in the circuit. There may be a fuse in the engine panel supply. More rarely, there may be a battery fuse on the battery itself, although this is, in fact, desirable.

The problem may be any one of the following:

- Any fuse in the starter or battery circuit

  – the panel will be 'dead'.

- The key-switch or button itself

  – if this is the problem, there will be no dimming of the panel lights as you try to start the engine.

- The starter relay

  – no dimming of the lights

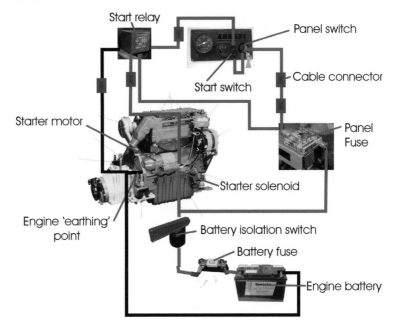

Only the wiring associated directly with the engine start
circuit is shown

- relay may or may not 'clunk', depending on which
  part has failed.

- The starter solenoid

  - no dimming of the lights

  - relay may or may not 'clunk', depending on which
    part has failed.

- Cable joints linking the components

  - a cable break can be found by the normal pro-
    cess

  - a corroded joint is more likely to be accompanied
    by a dimming of the panel lights

  - loose or corroded battery cables will cause dim-
    ming of lights – remember to check the negative
    cable joints, especially where one is clamped to
    the engine.

- The starter motor itself

  - panel lights may dim.

- Steel boats, and also some others, may have an isolating solenoid in the negative cable from the battery to the engine block. It's very easy to miss this.

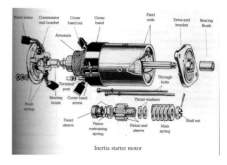

Inertia starter motor

Starter circuit problems

Old 'inertia-type' starter motors use a spiral shaft to propel the starter pinion to engage with the starter ring on the flywheel. The mechanic's solution to problems with this mechanism was pretty drastic. On these inertia starters, connecting the main terminals on the motor will cause the motor to run and the pinion to engage. This is not for the timid, as very high currents will flow, the screwdriver (or whatever is used to make the link) may become welded to the terminals and sparks will fly. It can be justified only in the most exceptional life-threatening circumstances.

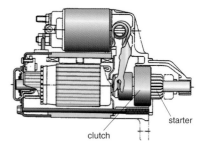

Sometimes the starter pinion sticks at the end of its travel and remains engaged with the flywheel starter ring. In this case, the starter motor has insufficient power to rotate the engine from standstill. The pinion can be wound back by applying a spanner to the squared end of the starter motor shaft (at the front of the starter) and rotating the shaft to disengage the pinion.

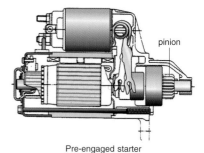

Pre-engaged starter

Modern 'pre-engaged' starter motors use a clutch to engage the pinion. Failure of the starter solenoid can't be overcome by linking the terminals, because the starter motor's clutch won't engage unless the solenoid operates.

The starter solenoid can be operated directly by applying 12 volts (or 24 volts) to the solenoid's input terminals. In fact, I have this system wired permanently in the engine compartment on my own boat, but with a hidden switch in the wire. This allows me to turn the engine over easily for maintenance purposes, as well as for emergency starting.

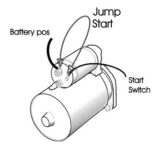

Hidden fuse revealed

Hidden fuse

Yanmar GM series starter circuits

These engines have multiple connectors in the wiring loom to the engine start panel. These are likely to corrode and the starter button may not always work – accompanied by dimming of the panel lights. These connectors will need to be cleaned (or bypassed) or a starter relay incorporated in the circuit.

Yanmar GM series engines also incorporate a panel fuse in the wiring harness, but hide it away.

Solenoid/relay problems

As well as the solenoid itself failing, the supply voltage or the signal voltage may have failed.

- Check the supply voltage (12 V or 24 V).

- Check the signal voltage when the starter switch is operated.

- You should hear or feel the solenoid (relay) operate.

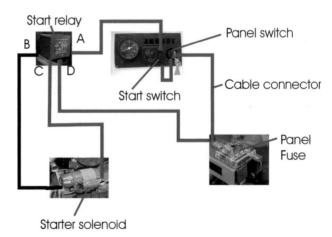

Start relay

B   A

C   D

Panel switch

Start switch

Cable connector

Panel Fuse

Starter solenoid

D - B (or any earthing point)   12 VOLTS (or 24 volts)

OPERATE STARTER SWITCH   A - B   12 VOLTS (or 24 volts)

(You should hear or feel   C - D   ZERO OHMS
a 'clunk')

Power circuit problems

Faultfinding in a power circuit is a very similar process to that used for a lighting circuit. Very heavy current devices, such as bow thrusters, windlasses and winches, will have a relay situated between the switch and the electric motor.

There is often a heavy-duty circuit breaker as well, so finding the fault will require a methodical approach working from one component to the next.

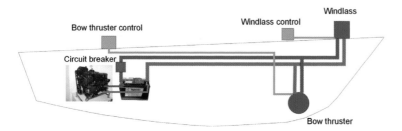

- Check that the panel circuit breaker has not tripped. The 'pop-out' button will be visible, or a rocker type will be off.

- Check the heavy-duty circuit breaker in the same way.

- Check the switch is working by checking continuity with the switch 'closed'. You will need access to the back of the switch so that you can use a multimeter to measure the resistance across the terminals – it should be close to zero ohms.

- Check the voltage across the relay's supply terminals (the terminals connected to the switch) when the switch is operated. The voltage should be close to 12 (or 24) volts.

- Check that the relay operates by listening for a 'click' or feeling a 'clunk'. You can also check the resistance across the output terminals with your multimeter – the resistance should be low, a couple of ohms or so.

- Check the supply voltage at the electric motor using your multimeter – it should be close to full-circuit voltage.

If all these checks are satisfactory, the problem is likely to be in the windlass/winch itself. Windlasses mounted in the chain locker are exposed to very damp conditions and corrosion can be a problem.

Foot-operated switches on the foredeck are also subject to corrosion, but some are actually air-pumps rather than switches. Compressing the bulb of the pump operates a remote pressure switch away from the wet foredeck. A leak in the bulb or pressure line will cause failure.

Water pressure pump fails to run

1. Check the fuse with a multimeter. As well as one on the panel, there may well be an in-line fuse in the supply wiring at the pump.

2. If the pump still does not run with at least one tap open, or fails to pump, then remove the wires from the pressure switch and join them together.

3. If the pump runs, the pressure switch is at fault.

Checking the pressure switch
It may be possible to check the pressure switch with the pump still mounted in position. If so:

1. Remove the pressure switch cover.

2. Push the micro switch button.

3. If the pump runs, the electrical switch is OK.

4. Push the pressure plunger to ensure that it moves in and out – it moves only about 2 or 3 mm but it should move. If it doesn't, it's seized and so can't operate the electrical switch. You will have to take the pump apart.

If you can't remove the cover with the pump in place, you will have to remove the pump:

1. Turn off the power to the pump.

2. Turn off the water supply, using a clamp if necessary.

3. Disconnect the wiring, undo the pipe work, remove mounting bolts/screws and remove the pump.

4. Reconnect the wires and switch the power back on.

5. Carry out steps 1 to 3 from the previous list of instructions.

If none of the steps above produces results, you will have to replace the pump.

Electric Motors and Alternators

ELECTRIC MOTORS

Electric motors on most modern pieces of marine equipment are not repairable, and the motor will need to be replaced. Water pumps, for example, have service kits to repair the pump, but a failure of the motor will need a new motor, although the rest of the pump can be retained.

Heavy-duty motors, such as an engine starter motor, windlass motor or bow thruster motor, may have the facility for replacing the 'brushes'. Where an electric current has to be supplied to a rotating component, carbon *brushes* bear on the rotating conductor as the shaft rotates. The brushes (there are two or more) will wear down and at some time will need replacing. Sets of new brushes, their conductor leads and pressure springs may be available to replace the worn set.

In the leisure marine environment, starter, windlass and winch motors get relatively little use, and brush failure is not very common.

Where replacement is possible, the equipment handbook will give details of how to do the job and also the part number of the spares kit required. The engine handbook will not give details of replacing starter motor brushes, but the workshop manual will. On some motors only a cover needs to be removed, but others need some disassembly to access the brushes.

A typical electric motor

The brushes may be hidden under a removable band around the motor, behind a plate at the end of the motor or under a deeper rear cover.

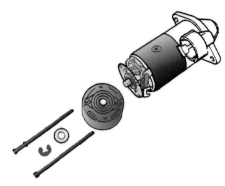

- *First, disconnect the battery.*

- Remove the main cables from the motor and also any signalling wires (solenoid), noting how they should be reconnected. (A starter motor may have no negative cable as this may be supplied via the engine block to which the motor is bolted.)

- Remove the motor from the unit.

- Remove the cap at the end of the motor. (1)

- Remove the 'C' shaped retainer on the end of the shaft. (2)

(1)

- Unscrew and remove the very long bolts holding the end cover in place. (3)

- Remove the end cover to access the brushes. (4)

- Remove the brushes from their holders – you will probably have to lever the springs out of the way using a small screwdriver. (5) & (6)

(2)

- Generally, starter motors have the brush cables soldered in place because they carry very high currents. Unsolder the brush cables with a soldering iron. Use a de-soldering tool to remove excess solder from the terminal – you'll need to keep the old solder molten with the iron while you use the vacuum de-soldering tool to suck the old solder away.

(3)

- Replace the brushes. This will vary from machine to machine – they will withdraw from the carrier after you have released the pressure on the spring.

- Reassemble the motor.

(4)  (5)  (6)

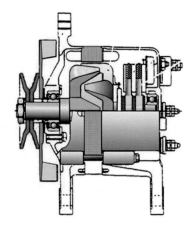

ALTERNATORS

A typical alternator

Like an electric motor, an alternator also has brushes, but these are usually hidden inside the casing and a degree of disassembly is required. Sometimes the brush conductor wire will need soldering in place. Alternator brushes suffer more wear than a leisure marine electric motor, but if an engine achieves only 100 hours a year, brush replacement is not likely to be required.

The engine handbook is unlikely to give details of how to change the brushes, but the workshop manual may.

The first job is to switch off the batteries and then disconnect their terminals so that there is no chance of any wire remaining 'live'. If you have the engine wiring diagram, reconnection of the wires will be no problem, but if not, make a sketch showing which wire goes where on the back of the alternator and then disconnect them all.

Some alternators, like the Lucas, have very easy access to the regulator and the brushes.

- Remove the alternator.

- Remove the two screws holding the cover in place. (7) & (8)

- Remove the screws holding the brush wires in place. (9)

- Remove the screws holding the brushes in place. (10) & (11)

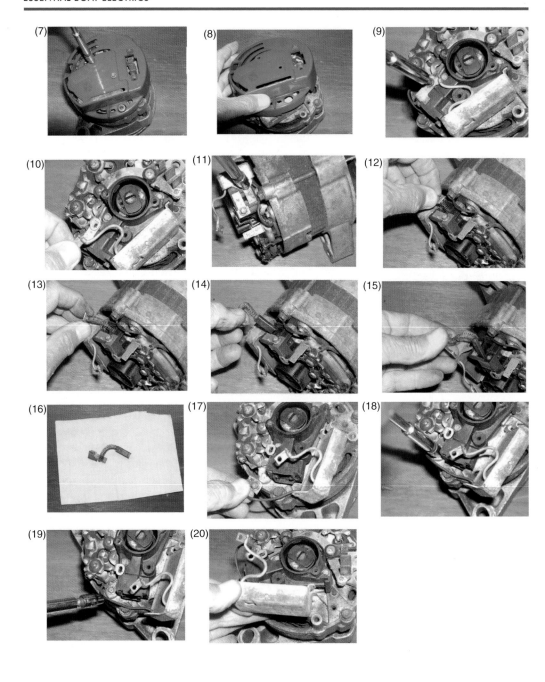

- Withdraw the brushes. (12)–(16)

- Detach the screw holding the regulator wire in place. (17), (18), (19)

- Detach the regulator. (20)

Other alternators, like the Hitachi fitted to Yanmar engines, require the alternator to be taken apart to get at the regulator and brushes. The sequence for fitting a smart regulator wire to a Hitachi is given in the next section.

Smart regulators

If a 'smart' regulator is to be fitted, some alternators, such as the Hitachi fitted to Yanmar engines, will need to have the field control wire soldered internally to allow the regulator to operate.

The first job is to switch off the batteries and then disconnect their terminals so that there is no chance of any wire remaining 'live'. If you have the engine wiring diagram, reconnection of the wires will be no problem, but if not, make a sketch showing which wire goes where on the back of the alternator and then disconnect them all.

- Undo the two bolts attaching the alternator and remove it to the workbench.

- Remove the five 10 mm nuts at the back of the alternator, noting that three of them have insulating spacers. It might be a good idea to mark the alternator showing which three studs need the insulators. In fact it is pretty obvious as these three have bigger holes in the casing. (21) & (22)

- The two halves of the casing are clamped together with four long screws and these must now be removed. (23)

- Carefully prise the front of the alternator casing from the stator (stationary coil assembly), working your way around the perimeter. (24), (25)

- Separate the alternator unit into its three main parts. (26)

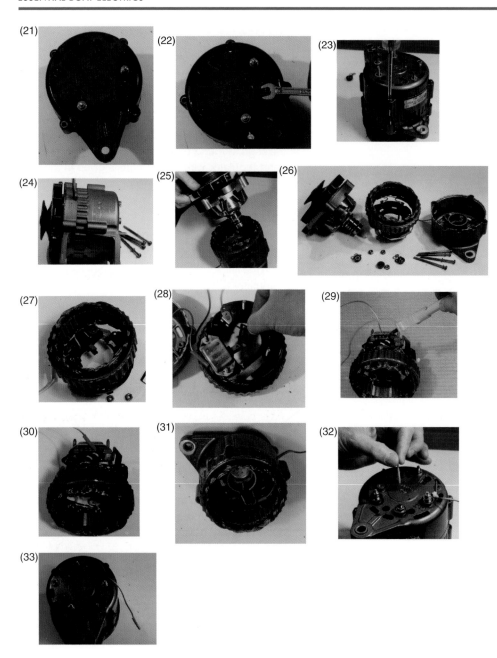

(21)

(22)

(23)

(24)

(25)

(26)

(27)

(28)

(29)

(30)

(31)

(32)

(33)

- You now have access to the stator, rectifier pack, standard regulator and the brush assembly. (27)

- Solder the new wire onto the regulator field terminal, as identified in the instructions (it should be marked 'F'). (29)

- Slip an insulating sleeve in place. (30)

- Note the carbon brushes and the rectangular brush assembly seal. (28)

- All is now ready for reassembly.

- Thread the new wire through the rear of the casing in such a way that it will not foul anything inside, and so that you can clip it to a slot with a cable tie. Put the brush assembly seal in place and slip the stator assembly into the rear casing, making sure that the seal is seated correctly. (31)

- In this figure a match has been inserted into a hole in the back of the case to hold the brushes in a retracted position prior to the insertion of the rotor. A match was used for clarity in the picture, but is not really strong enough to do the job. A suitable drill bit would be better. (32)

- Offer up the front casing and guide the bearing and armature gently into place. If any untoward resistance is felt, start again and check that the brushes are fully retracted, as they are easily damaged. Don't force it into place!

- Withdraw the drill bit and reassemble all the spacers, washers and nuts.

- Attach a connector to the new wire and you are ready to reinstall the alternator. (33)

- Tension the drive belt correctly and ensure the attachment bolts are secure. Complete the external wiring using the smart regulator's wiring diagram and you are ready to sample the pleasures of fully charged batteries.

The first time I did this, the work on the alternator took half an hour. The second time, to take some more pictures, took only 10 minutes!

Navigation
Instruments

M odern boats have an array of instrumentation, sometimes fitted after delivery or as an upgrade on older boats.

The wiring-up of instruments often leaves much to be desired. Instruments may switch themselves off during engine start – see the section on 12 volt DC circuits on p. 37 for avoidance of this problem. The installer should provide a wiring diagram of the installation, but this is a rarity.

Avoid in-line fuses to individual instruments. Faultfinding is much easier if fuses are grouped together in an accessible 'fuse centre', not hidden away behind a panel. Again, this is a rarity.

Instruments should be sited where they are of most use to the helmsman/navigator. This is very often not at the chart table, but in the cockpit. Unless there is a dedicated navigator, radar and chart-plotters should be sited where they can be seen by the helmsman/ skipper.

INTERCONNECTION OF INSTRUMENTS

The North American Marine Electronics Association (NMEA) has devised a language understood by instruments from many manufacturers, so that those instruments can talk to each other. The current version (2004) is NMEA 0183 v 2.3. Manufacturers do sometimes add 'sentences' of their own, but generally compatibility is good.

This enables you to choose different instruments from different manufacturers, according to your preference, and for the most part they will all interact together properly. However, sometimes they don't and you may get some 'buck-passing' between the manufacturers. You may find it preferable to get all the instruments from one dealer and specify in the order that you want them all to work together in the same system. If there's a problem, it's much more likely that your dealer will have success in getting an answer than you will.

Each manufacturer will normally have an 'in-house' language for its own instruments, in addition to NMEA. This is because they can achieve a faster communication speed and because they can develop special procedures without waiting for a committee to catch up. This has become especially so now that chart-plotters can show radar and fish-finder images at the same time.

Instruments from the same manufacturer

This is the simplest option, both from the wiring and compatibility points of view. They will be guaranteed to work together.

A single cable 'daisy chains' all the instruments together, and extra instruments can be connected at any time. This cable carries both data and power, and joints are made with simple plugs and sockets. The only extra cables are those to aerials (GPS, radio and radar) and transducers (speed and depth).

If you like the instruments from one manufacturer's range, this is a good way to go.

Sometimes, a particular range of instruments does not include one particular instrument, a radar, say. Adding only one 'foreign' instrument is not usually a problem, but do ask the supplying dealer first.

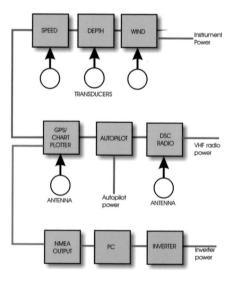

ALL NAVIGATION INSTRUMENTS OF SAME MAKE

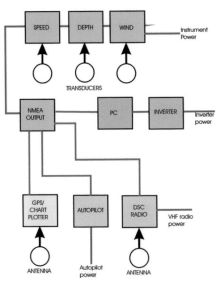

MIXTURE OF MAKES OF INSTRUMENTS

Instruments from different manufacturers

Some makes will need an NMEA converter to be added to the system, but most newer instruments will have an NMEA output as standard. Wires will be required to connect each instrument, and wiring colour-coding will often differ. Careful thought must be given to the way in which the instruments will be interconnected, especially where a chart-plotter and GPS are connected to other instruments.

It's very easy to make a real tangle of wires if you are interconnecting a lot of instruments, unless a lot of thought and preparation is made.

- Start by making a wiring diagram.

- Consider where the connectors are to be sited – all in one place is best, but that may mean longer wiring runs.

- If possible, make up a circuit board with wiring connectors to take wires to each instrument.

Nylon connection blocks are not ideal for connecting small-gauge signal wires, and joint failures are likely.

MULTIPLEXERS

If instruments from many manufacturers are to be incorporated, it would be sensible to install a multiplexer. In this, all the different NMEA sentences are fed into the multiplexer, combined, and a single multiplex signal containing all the data is sent back out to all the instruments requiring it. This avoids a lot of problems. Multiplexers may be obtained from ACTISENSE (www.actisense.com).

INSTALLATION OF INSTRUMENTS

Where you fit the instrument displays is very important. Left to his own devices, the boat builder or instrument installer will put the instruments in traditional places, often at the chart table. Consider how and when the instruments will be used. If you usually sail short-handed, then the main instruments need to be in the helmsman's sight and preferably reach.

However, mounting all the instruments on the binnacle means that the rest of the crew is kept out of the picture, so mounting them further forward in the cockpit has distinct advantages.

Although instruments these days are declared to be waterproof, often the connectors at the rear of the display are not. If this is the case, then the display must be mounted so that its rear is protected. A box can be built to achieve this.

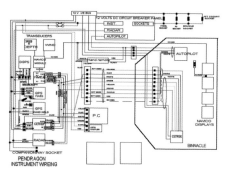

PENDRAGON
INSTRUMENT WIRING

Instruments in motor cruisers or boats with dual steering positions need just as much careful consideration as those fitted in the cockpit of a sailing boat.

- Where will you be helming from when you need that particular instrument?

- What instrumentation do you need at *both* stations?

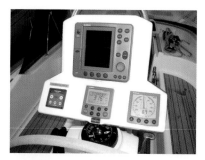

- Does the instrument need to be seen by more than one person at the same time?

- Will the siting cause reflections in the windscreen at night? (some installations make it impossible to see through the windscreen at night, due to reflections from the instrument lighting!)

Make a mock up of the instrument layout before you cut holes in the boat!

PCs

I shall not be considering the use of a PC on board, only its wiring.

Power supply

Laptop PCs

These use a mains adapter to supply a suitable DC voltage. The problem is that this voltage varies, even in one manufacturer's range, so if you provide a built-in supply on the boat, it probably will be unsuitable for your next computer. For this reason, I use an inverter to supply 240 AC from my 12 volt system and run my computer from this using its dedicated mains adapter. Electrically this is not the most efficient arrangement, but it's kinder on the pocket when you change PCs.

An average laptop computer will draw around 4 amps from a 12 volt DC supply. This is roughly equivalent to the current taken by a fridge.

Desktop PCs

These are designed to run on mains AC voltage, although there are several 'marine' units that will run on 12 volts DC. Those requiring mains voltage can be run on shore power, an inverter or an on-board generator.

An average mains-powered desktop computer will draw up to 30 amps from a 12 volt DC system. For the average yachtsman who may want to use his computer under way, this is far too much current and is not a practicable proposition.

Normally, an inverter of sufficient power to run a desktop PC will be 'built-in' and the battery drain will be significant. I have seen a PC shut down because the battery voltage became too low, causing the inverter to switch itself off. This happened several times, and the owner had to accept that he would need to run his genset when using the computer. As he was going to use his computer for navigation, this was a definite disadvantage. He ended up buying a laptop computer as well! In any case, the hard drive in a laptop is much more rugged than that in a desktop.

Connection to instruments

For use in navigation, your computer will need to be connected so that it can receive NMEA data via its serial or USB port. Most new laptops have no serial port, so it will probably need to be a USB connection. Currently, most NMEA data cables terminate in a serial connector, so you will need a serial/USB adapter.

It is preferable to use an 'opto-isolator' data cable to prevent voltage spikes upsetting the computer or NMEA data bus.

If you have more than about four instruments being supplied from a single NMEA source, you may have to fit an NMEA *buffer* to amplify the signals and provide sufficient output for the computer. This buffer will need a 12 volt power supply, as well as the NMEA input.

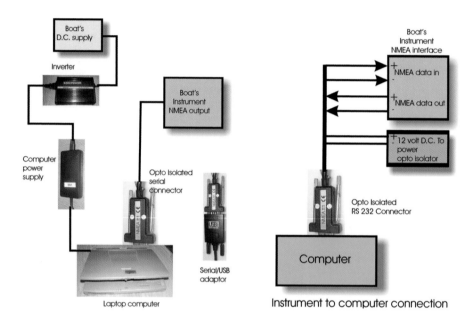

Laptop computer

Instrument to computer connection

NMEA/computer connection

The connector will be supplied with a colour-coded diagram to aid connection to the boat's NMEA interface.

Siting the computer

Many people place their computer on the chart table. It is then susceptible to spray entering the companionway and also to being lent on by people wearing wet foul-weather gear or being operated by wet hands.

I use mine set up vertically on an open cupboard door, with operation by a remote mouse or tracker ball. A sacrificial cheap keyboard, or even a waterproof keyboard, may be used as well.

INSTRUCTIONS
To assemble PL259.

1. Unscrew the two parts of the plug and slide the barrel onto the cable.

2. Cut back outer sheath for 30mm **A**.

3. Cut back 25mm of the braid **B** revealing the dielectric.

4. Tease out the braid and fold back over the outer sheath as in **C**.

5. Now carefully remove 20mm of the dielectric and tin the conductor **D**.

6. Carefully screw the plug onto the cable until the folded back screen just disappears inside the plug. Don't go further or you could cause a short circuit.

7. Solder conductor into the prong and snip off any excess **E**. Then screw the barrel onto the plug.

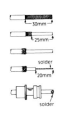

Courtesy of Index Marine.

INSTRUCTIONS
To assemble BNC connector.

Slide the clamp nut and plain gasket onto the cable **A**. Then cut back approx. 10mm of the outer sheath **B** exposing the braid **C**. Tease out the braid **D** and then cut it right back to the outer sheath **E** exposing the dielectric conductor cover. Then slide the ferrule over the dielectric and under the braid **F**. Using a sharp knife, trim the dielectric right back to the face of the ferrule **G** thus exposing the conductor which now should be tinned. Cut the conductor back so that 4mm is left showing, then assemble the plug in the order shown in **A1** making sure that the contact pin is soldered

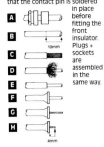

in place before fitting the front insulator. Plugs + sockets are assembled in the same way.

COMMUNICATIONS RADIOS

VHF radio

A VHF radio is capable of transmitting at 25 watts. This requires a good power supply fused at around 7.5 amps, with cable heavy enough to cause minimum voltage drop. Generally, this means 2.5 mm² cable.

No matter how good the radio, a poor antenna installation will give poor transmissions. All antenna cable joints must be properly made and kept to a minimum, and the antenna itself must be correctly sited. Follow the manufacturer's guidance.

The radio may transmit perfectly well on 1 watt, but at the full 25 watts power, transmission will be poor or non-existent with a poor antenna. Reception is no indication of antenna performance, even though the transmitting station may be some distance away. Poor antenna connections can cause failure of the transmitter's output circuit, as can transmitting with no antenna connected.

In order to check the antenna installation, you need a standing wave ratio (SWR) meter.

All professional installers will have one, but one suitable for use by the boat owner is available for around £20 from a radio spares supplier. Without going into technicalities, an SWR meter measures how much of the signal is sent back down the cable rather than being transmitted. It is the only way to check an antenna installation, and instructions for its use will be supplied with the meter.

It has to be said that the majority of radio installers will not use an SWR meter to check the installation, and nor will they check the DSC operation of a DSC radio to ensure that the DSC is actually working. Only if a problem is reported will they delve deeper.

Connection of a DSC radio to a GPS

A DSC radio requires a position input from a GPS. As there is no full standardisation of the NMEA wiring colours, you will need to check the colour of the NMEA data outputs of your instrument system. Normally there will be a data +ve and a data −ve wire.

HF radio

Power supply and antenna connections are very important with an HF radio installation, as is the antenna itself.

In the long-distance cruising fraternity, it seems to be generally accepted that good performance of an HF radio installation is best achieved by a professional familiar with HF installation.

Anodes

CATHODIC PROTECTION

Sea water is an electrolyte, just as the liquid in your battery is an electrolyte. It will allow current to flow between two metal fittings immersed in the electrolyte if those fittings have different electrical potentials and they are connected together electrically.

Different metals will have differing electrical potentials when connected together and immersed in sea water. Their potential can be found on an anodic table of potentials, and in extreme cases they may be separated by as much as 1.5 volts. The metal at the higher voltage will be eaten away, and if the potential difference is greater than 0.25 volts, corrosion is almost certain to occur.

This all sounds a bit complicated, and indeed there are specialists in electrolytic corrosion, as the process is called, such as M.G. Duff. As far as a book such as this is concerned, what we need to know is how to protect vulnerable hull fittings. There's a little bit more on this topic in the section on A.C. circuits on p. 43.

Essentially, when used in sea water, external hull fittings are protected by a zinc *anode* wired into the same circuit as the fittings. The anode gives up zinc in order to protect the fittings themselves from corrosion. Indeed, these anodes are normally referred to as *sacrificial* anodes, because they sacrifice themselves.

To a lesser extent, electrolytic corrosion can occur in fresh and brackish water. In fresh water, the anode is made of magnesium. For use in brackish water, ideally use aluminium. Be guided by what other people use in that area.

ANODES

An anode must be fitted as close as possible to the fitting that it is protecting, and it must be connected to it electrically. On a glass fibre hull, the main protection is needed by the stern gear: the propshaft, 'P' bracket (if fitted) and the propeller. A steel rudder stock may also need protection. The anode must be able to 'see' all these components and be wired to them. This means mounting the anode as close as possible to the fitting and with no intervening structure.

In Europe, the other skin fittings are rarely included in the anodic circuit, but in the USA, they often are. Because the sea water cooling intake is connected to the engine by the sea water in the hose, Westerly Yachts always had their cooling intake included in the anodic circuit. Wooden boats should not have their skin fittings bonded, because if they are, the wood surrounding the fitting will become softened.

The anode is bolted to the outside of the hull using special studs. Internally, the studs are connected to the engine block and the 'P' bracket and to the rudder stock, if necessary, by heavy copper wires run out of the bilges

There needs to be electrical continuity all the way from the anode to the propeller shaft and prop (and any other fitting to be protected). The resistance from the anode to the prop should not exceed a couple of ohms. If the propeller shaft coupling at the rear of the gearbox electrically isolates the shaft from the engine, some form of electrical bridge needs to be provided. This can be in the form of an electrical strap across the coupling, or electrical *brushes* bearing on the shaft.

- All connections must be kept clean and corrosion-free.

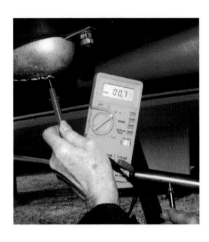

- New nuts and fan washers should be used each time the anode is changed.
- Wire can become corroded.
- If the anode is not eroding, it's probably not connected!
- Test for continuity with the multimeter. Ideally, resistance should be no more than a couple of ohms, but multimeters may not be too accurate at very small resistance readings.
- Use your long multimeter probe lead to check the resistance from the 'bonding' cable to the external anode (outside, not its bolt).
- Check for continuity from the anode to the propshaft, propeller and the 'P' bracket.

Propellers mounted on rubber bushes

Some propellers are mounted on rubber bushes so there can then be no continuity between any anode and the propeller. The prop is then protected from dezincification only by its own propeller anode. This is often very small and may not last the season, so it will need to be inspected mid-season.

Very corroded saildrive leg anode

Volvo Penta saildrives

The latest models of Volvo Penta compact saildrive engines have their gearboxes electrically isolated from their engines. On these engines, on no account must there be any electrical bridge between the two. Check your handbook to see if your engine/gearbox is isolated. Protection of the propeller and leg is provided solely by the leg anode.

With a standard prop, the anode will just about last a year. Folding props with heavy bosses may need to have the anode replaced mid-season to avoid corrosion of the prop.

This prop hub is already showing signs of dezincification through electrolytic corrosion. Note that a reddish colour indicates surface dezincification.

Suspended anodes

Where extra anodic protection is needed, a hanging anode can be suspended in the water close to where the protection is required. This anode is sometimes called a *guppy*. The anode is connected electrically to a wire, the other end of which is clipped to a component that is electrically connected to a fitting in the 'bonding' circuit. For example, the ground circuit could be extended by connecting a bonding wire to a cockpit fitting, and the guppy cable could be clipped to this as required. If the saildrive leg is electrically isolated, ensure that the guppy is connected to the gearbox and not to the engine.

Steel hulls

The steel from which the hull is built also needs to be protected by anodes, the siting of which should be determined with the help of a specialist, such as M.G. Duff.

Aluminium hulls

Aluminium hulls or superstructures can be wasted away within months if electrolytic currents are set up. This is a very specialist area and thus advice from one of these specialists is mandatory.

Aluminium anodes

Recently launched by Performance Metals (www.performancemetals.com) is a series of aluminium/indium alloy anodes. These work equally well in fresh, brackish and sea water, and they work immediately after relaunching.

Aluminium/indium is lighter than zinc and also 0.05 volts less noble, so it gives more protection for aluminium and steel than does zinc. Importantly, it is claimed to have 40% greater life than zinc.

Protecting aluminium stern-drives against electrolytic corrosion is particularly difficult, and aluminium/indium anodes could bring significant gains over using zinc anodes.

GROUND PLATES

Some radio and navigation receivers and transmitters require a 'ground plane' if they are to give satisfactory performance. This requires a large metallic surface immersed below the water. One way to achieve this is to connect the ground circuit to the iron keel. A better way is to use a 'sintered' bronze *ground plate* attached to the exterior of the hull below the waterline

The ground plate is full of minute holes and fissures so that its actual surface area is much greater than it would seem. The ground plate is electrically connected to the electrical ground of the boat's DC system.

Soldering

Soldering is the technique of joining two metals together by melting another metal onto their surfaces as a form of 'adhesive'. Soldering doesn't fuse the metals together as in welding.

For joining copper electrical wires, we use a solder of tin/lead alloy, which has a relatively low melting temperature.

The process of soldering causes oxidisation on the surfaces to be joined, and this prevents adhesion of the solder to the other metal surfaces. For this reason, a *flux* has to be applied to prevent oxidisation. For our purposes, the easiest way to do this is to use proprietary *multicore* solder, where an acid-free flux ('rosin flux') is stored in minute cores within the solder, which is provided in the form of a wire.

SOLDERING IRONS

The heat to melt the solder is provided by a soldering iron. The size and power of the iron are important. There should be only enough heat to raise the temperature sufficiently in the region of the joint. Too much heat may cause damage to adjacent areas, such as the wire's insulation; too little, and the solder will not melt.

Small electronic components, such as transistors and diodes, will be destroyed by too much heat, and even the smallest iron will be too big. To get over this problem, a temporary *heat sink* is attached to the wire between the component and the soldering iron, and soldering should be accomplished quickly using a hot iron. The heat sink draws excessive heat away from the delicate component. A small crocodile clip with sufficient mass will do the job.

For most boat wiring, a 25 watt iron, or its equivalent, will be fine. For soldering heavy-duty cables, this will be insufficient, but soldering may not be the best method of joining heavier cable anyway.

The size of the tip should be appropriate for the size of the job to be tackled.

On the boat, a 12 volt iron is very useful.

If mains voltage is available, a 25 watt mains-powered iron can be used, although a second, larger iron of up to 100 watts can be useful for some bigger jobs.

A gas-powered soldering iron is very versatile, as it can be used for cutting, heat-shrinking and sealing rope as well. A word of warning here: I have found that the catalytic heater of cheaper gas irons lasts for a very short time. Since using a more expensive 'professional' iron I have had no such problems.

SOLDERING TECHNIQUE

Soldering is not at all difficult, but a bit of practice helps.

- Switch on the iron and allow it to achieve its full temperature. This can be checked by touching the solder to the tip to check that the solder melts.

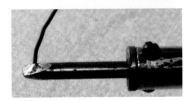

- Clean the tip of the iron on a damp cloth or sponge.

- Apply a small amount of solder to the hot tip in order to *tin* it.

- If the tip has become burned and pock-marked, restore its condition using a file.

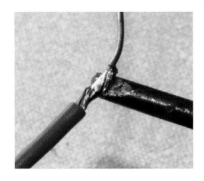

- The surfaces of the area to be soldered must be clean and free of corrosion – this means they must be bright.

- The surfaces must be *tinned* before making the joint – this is the application of a thin layer of solder to the areas to be joined. Heat the wire with the iron, and with the iron still in contact with the wire, melt some solder onto the wire. Then repeat for the second wire.

- Hold the two wires together and apply heat. The tinning should melt and join the wires together. If necessary, apply more solder wire to the joint, not to the iron's tip.

- The resultant joint should be bright and shiny. If it has a dull, crinkled look, it was not hot enough or the joint was moved before it had cooled – this is known as a dry joint. It will have high electrical resistance and poor mechanical strength and must be remade.

Some form of clamping may be required if you run out of hands! It's also very useful to have a holder in which to safely rest the hot soldering iron.

Heavy-duty joints

Soldering heavy cables may be achieved by using a gas blowtorch, as used for plumbing. There's a big danger of melting the wire's insulation and a better option is (usually) crimping using a professional heavy-duty crimping tool.

MECHANICAL STRENGTH

Soldered joints must not be relied upon to give mechanical strength. Support the wire on either side of the joint.

If more mechanical strength is desirable, twist the wires together before tinning them and then make the joint. This will be difficult to unsolder if you need to break the joint.

Some electrical components have a lug with a hole in it, to which the wire is soldered. Loop the bared untinned wire through the lug. Now heat the lug and wire with the hot iron and apply the solder to the wire AND the lug together to make the joint. If you don't twist the wire, it will not be difficult to unsolder.

UNSOLDERING JOINTS

It is sometimes much easier to undo a soldered joint if most of the solder is first removed. To do this you need a de-soldering tool.

- Heat the joint so that the solder melts.

- Apply the tip of the tool to the hot joint and suck off the melted solder.

- Reheat the joint, which should then be easy to undo.

If you don't have a de-soldering tool, melt the solder and pull the joint apart. If there's a lug with a hole, the hole will immediately fill up with solder again, so if you are going to remake the joint, try and wipe the solder off with a wet rag – it's better to buy the correct tool if you are going to tackle this sort of job.

Power Consumption

Everybody's electrical power needs are different. What you need to do is examine your sailing lifestyle and make an attempt to assess how much electricity you are going to use, on average, each day.

To that end, I've made an attempt to guess what the average boater might use in various conditions, so that you can adapt my figures to your type of boating. The numbers are for a 12 volt system. If yours is 24 volts, the amps and Ah/day will be halved. See the tables on pages 34–36 for reference.

A modern cruiser could easily consume 115 Ah for a 12-hour passage under sail. Frugal use of electrical power could reduce this to 35 Ah.

The picture differs somewhat if we are at anchor or moored without recourse to shore power.

On a modern cruiser, 24 hours moored could typically consume 80 Ah. Frugal use of power could reduce this to 35 Ah per day. Additionally, if a diesel-powered heater is used, expect to consume 4 Ah per hour running.

If we have access to shore power, then the picture changes radically.

What is not obvious in this last case is that we may also need to charge our depleted batteries. In the case above, we are using 14 amps DC current, which must come from the battery charger, so if we've a 30 amp battery charger, only 16 is going into the battery to charge it up. Taking into account charging efficiency and other factors, that's going to take around 16 hours to fully charge our batteries if we need to put 200 Ah back in.

An additional consideration is that the total possible AC load far exceeds the amperage of the 240 volt power supply. Although an overload should trip our on-board circuit breaker first, we could trip the pontoon breaker. That may make us very unpopular with our neighbours, as often this breaker can be reset only by marina staff.

USEFUL TABLES

BATTERY STATE OF CHARGE	BATTERY VOLTS			
	RESTED	0 AMPS	5 AMPS	10 AMPS
100%	12.8	12.5	12.4	12.2
90%	12.7	12.4	12.3	12.1
80%	12.6	12.3	12.2	12.0
70%	12.5	12.2	12.1	11.9
60%	12.4	12.1	12.0	11.8
50%	12.3	12.0	11.9	11.7
40%	12.2	11.9	11.8	11.6
30%	12.1	11.8	11.7	11.5
20%	12.0	11.7	11.6	
10%	11.9	11.6		
FLAT	11.8	11.5		

BATTERY STATE OF CHARGE

MINIMUM WIRE SIZES

Wire sizes required for a given length of cable run (Length is the sum of the positive and negative wires)

Wire size 3% voltage drop (Critical applications – bilge pumps, nav. lights, electronics, etc.)

LENGTH	CURRENT (amps)								
	5 a	10 a	15 a	20 a	25 a	30 a	40 a	50 a	100 a
5 m	16	12	10	10	8	8	6	6	2
10 m	12	10	8	6	6	4	4	2	1/0
20 m	10	6	6	4	2	2	1	1/0	4/0
30 m	8	4	4	2	1	1/0	2/0	3/0	
40 m	6	4	2	1	1/0	2/0	3/0	4/0	
50 m	6	2	1	1/0	2/0	3/0	4/0		

Wire size 10% voltage drop (Non-critical applications – windlasses, cabin lights, etc.)

LENGTH	CURRENT (amps)								
	5 a	10 a	15 a	20 a	25 a	30 a	40 a	50 a	100 a
5 m	18	18	16	16	14	14	12	12	6
10 m	18	16	14	12	10	10	8	8	4
20 m	16	12	10	8	8	8	6	4	2
30 m	14	10	8	8	6	6	4	4	1
40 m	12	8	8	6	4	4	2	2	2/0
50 m	10	8	6	4	4	2	2	1	3/0

American wire gauge 'boat cable'

AWG	18	16	14	12	10	8	6	4	2	1	1/0	2/0	3/0	4/0
mm²		0.8	1	2	3	5	8	13	19	32	40	50	62	81	103
Max. amps	20	25	35	45	60	80	120	160	210	245	285	330	385	445

Reduce current by 15% when run in engine compartment.

Standard UK wire sizes – 1, 1.5, 2.5, 4, 6, 25 and 40 mm².

GALVANIC CORROSION TABLE

METAL	POTENTIAL volts
Magnesium alloys	−1.6
Galvanised iron	−1.05
Zinc	−1.03
Cadmium	−0.8
Alumnium alloys	−0.75
Mild steel	−0.65
Lead	−0.55
Type 304 stainless steel(A2) (active - oxgen starved)	−0.53
Copper	−0.36
Admiralty brass	−0.29
Manganese bronze	−0.27
Slicon bronze	−0.18
Type 316 stainless steel(A4) (active - oxygen (starved)	−0.18
Inconel	−0.17
Titanium	−0.15
Silver	−0.13
Type 304 stainless steel(A2) (passive)	−0.08
Monel	−0.08
Type 316 stainless steel(A4) (passive)	−0.05
Platinum	+0.21
Graphite	+0.25

See page 125, chapter 12

You rely on us.
Can we rely on you?

Become an Offshore member
from just £5 a month.

Last year, our volunteers rescued over 8000 people but we couldn't have rescued a single one of them without the support of people like you. Join Offshore today, and you'll be helping to run the Lifeboat service whose volunteers will be on hand, should you ever get into difficulty at sea

Please call **0800 543210** quoting 'FB06'
or visit **rnli.org.uk**

Charity registered in England, number 209603

Offshore